A PLUME BOOK

LAST MAN OFF

MATT LEWIS is a trained marine biologist with an MSc with distinction in Marine and Fisheries Science. He now lives with his wife and two children near Aberdeen, Scotland.

Praise for *Last Man Off*

"A story that reminds us of the unforgiving nature of the sea and the courage that lies within the everyday heroes that have found themselves in hell."

—Bear Grylls

"Reads like a sinister version of *The Perfect Storm* . . . Thrilling, compelling, unsettling, rewarding."

—*The Sunday Times* (London)

"A dramatic tale of survival in one of the most brutal situations on earth. Feels like reading the diary of a doomed man . . . so personal and chillingly real; totally takes you there in a way that is not always comfortable."

—Steve Backshall

"A heart-thumping tale of tragedy and survival—minus the Hollywood ending . . . page-turning pace, compelling."

—*Daily Telegraph* (London)

"One of the most dramatic true-life tales of endurance and survival in recent memory. Should take its place alongside *The Perfect Storm* as a chilling account of how a fishing trip can go fatally awry. Unflinching and gripping, simultaneously terrifying and stirring."

—*The Observer* (London)

LAST MAN OFF

A True Story of Disaster and Survival
on the Antarctic Seas

MATT LEWIS

A PLUME BOOK

PLUME
Published by the Penguin Group
Penguin Group (USA) LLC
375 Hudson Street
New York, New York 10014

USA | Canada | UK | Ireland | Australia | New Zealand | India | South Africa | China
penguin.com
A Penguin Random House Company

Published by Plume, a member of Penguin Group (USA) LLC, 2015
Originally published in Great Britain by Viking, 2014

ISBN 978-0-14-751534-6

Printed in the United States of America
1   3   5   7   9   10   8   6   4   2

For the boys

CONTENTS

PART III: ADRIFT

PART IV: DELIVERANCE

AUTHOR'S NOTE

This book is my attempt to record an event that took place in June 1998 during the winter in the Southern Ocean. I was a Scientific Observer aboard the *Sudur Havid*, a South African deep-sea fishing boat, and it was my first job since graduating from university as a marine biologist.

Outside South Africa, the fate of the *Sudur Havid* was never big news. It was just another foreign fishing boat in trouble. Really, I should be calling her the *Sudurhavid*, or even *Suðurhavið*, for I have come to learn that this was her proper name. But on board I only ever saw the word split on life-rings, and I've known her as the *Sudur Havid* for far too long to change. To continue with the confessional, I have used the more familiar term 'Antarctic Seas' for the subtitle of the book when we were technically only 54° South – but we were south of the Antarctic convergence, so the water masses and ecology are much the same.

I waited a long time before I started writing *Last Man Off*. Partly this was due to a lack of self-belief, but it was also because I was trying to get on with my life and forget. I was trying to persuade myself that nothing of any significance had happened, so to write a book about the events was the last thing on my mind.

I'm glad I waited to start writing. In the immediate aftermath of the accident I was so caught up in being a participant, and there was so much emotion, that it was impossible to be objective in description. When the police in the Falkland Islands asked me what had happened, I barely paused for breath for three hours, producing sixty-five pages of descriptions, times and details. I kept the transcript of the interview and, eight years later, this and other evidence helped me relive and reconstruct the events. By that time the need to blame had mellowed, I had listened to others as they discussed what had happened, and processed the events myself. Time passed has made the story clearer, and less painful to tell.

There was coverage of the *Sudur Havid* in Cape Town. Some accounts were based on fact, some were more like fiction, but none were complete. I slipped quietly back into the UK, no cameras or journalists waiting for me at the airport, and I was grateful. My friends and family let me be; they didn't want to drag up traumatic memories, and assumed that I would talk about things in my own time. But I didn't want to tell those I cared about for fear of scaring them, and didn't tell others for fear of upsetting myself. It took years for me to realize that there was a story that deserved to be known. How could the struggle of a crew against the toughest seas in the world have slipped by? While I have been writing, a number of my fellow survivors have died, leaving the biggest story of their lives untold.

I knew that I would need to describe events that I had not directly witnessed. After years out of touch, I managed to make contact with Phil Marshall of the *Isla Camila* and Magnus Johnson from the *Northern Pride*, and met to interview them. For Phil, in particular, the memories were upsetting. It wasn't pleasant to ask him to recall as much detail as I needed, but he helped me to describe the search and the moment of rescue.

As the book took shape, and I became more committed, I travelled to South Africa to interview some of the crew. In a series of one-on-one interviews, I checked my recollections with Morné Van Geems, Sven Lizamore and Stephan Truter from the *Sudur Havid*, and they described events I couldn't have witnessed in the other raft. There were small conflicts between their memories and mine, but I expected this. They also helped me to build up a better picture of the techniques that we used in fishing, which was something I wanted to describe as vividly as I could. We sat and chatted in the shade, outside their comfortable Cape Town homes, and their stories took me back to the Southern Ocean. Their enthusiasm and drive to fish still humble and mystify me; they are fishermen to the core. By the end of the book I had also been helped by Big Danie from the *Sudur Havid*, and finally Captain Ernesto Sandoval from the *Isla Camila*.

Writing has not been the healing process I had hoped for; I have been reduced to tears on many occasions. It has been less of a catharsis and more of a self-imposed torture as I have forced myself to picture and relive painful events, again and again. I am fearful of misportraying men who were operating under great stress, and know that for some I am describing the deaths of loved ones.

I wish I had more photos, which would make the boat and the people more vivid for you and for me. But my camera is still on the *Sudur Havid*. Port side, aft cabin, on the main deck, in the right-hand drawer under my bunk. If anyone wants to get it for me, it's at 53°56′S, 041°30′W.

The surprise for me, in writing, was realizing how much I miss the sea, the boat and the adventure. For a short time in the Southern Ocean, I was at my most alive, at my best.

CREW LIST: MFV *SUDUR HAVID*

NAME	POSITION	HOME COUNTRY
Bjorgvin Armannsson	Captain	Iceland
Gerard (Bubbles) McDonagh	Skipper	South Africa
Brian (Boetie) Kuttel	Fishing Master	South Africa
Klaus Irmer	Chief Engineer	Germany
Glanville (Glen) Petersen	Second Engineer	South Africa
Joaquim Texeira	Deck Bosun	Portugal
João Carlos Mangas Santos	Factory Bosun	Portugal
Charlie Baron	Factory Bosun	South Africa
Matt Lewis	Scientific Observer	United Kingdom
Kenneth (Kenny) Adams	Deckhand	South Africa
Albert Baron	Deckhand	South Africa
Alfred (Alfie) Clarke	Deckhand	South Africa
Alexander Efeinge	Deckhand	South Africa
Trevor Fell	Deckhand	South Africa
Brian Forbes	Deckhand	South Africa
Grant Forbes	Deckhand	South Africa
Danie (Big Danie) Greeff	Deckhand	South Africa
Matheus Haimbodi	Deckhand	Namibia
Jerimia Kashingola	Deckhand	Namibia
Matheus Kashingola	Deckhand	Namibia
Antonio Kelobi	Deckhand	Namibia
David Knowles	Deckhand	South Africa
Sven Lizamore	Deckhand	South Africa

Eugene Nieman	Deckhand	South Africa
Joshua Peinge	Deckhand	South Africa
Stephan Truter	Deckhand	South Africa
Kanime Vahongaifa	Deckhand	Namibia
Morné Van Geems	Deckhand	South Africa
Mark Van Vuuren	Deckhand	South Africa
Inmamuel Vendadu	Deckhand	Namibia
Johannes (Hannes) Visser	Deckhand	South Africa
Samuel Walu Walu	Deckhand	South Africa
Daniel (Little Danie) Joubert	Deckhand/Greaser	South Africa
Melvin Marais	Electrician	South Africa
Alfius Shikonga	Greaser	Namibia
Gideon Dyson	Galley Boy	South Africa
Obiator (Simon) Shinana	Steward	Namibia
Robert (Grunter) Stevens	Chief Cook	South Africa

GLOSSARY

bosun   foreman of the crew on deck.

bow   the front end of the ship.

deck-suit   a waterproof but unsealed suit that can be worn for everyday work on deck. A layer of foam insulation adds buoyancy in the event of a fall overboard.

derrick   a crane with a moving, pivoted arm for hoisting objects on deck or out of the hold.

dogs   the metal levers that close and lock a waterproof storm door, clamping it shut.

engine casing   the metal structure that houses the upper parts of the engine room and the exhaust pipes.

EPIRB   Emergency Position-Indicating Radio Beacon. Self-contained, individually identifiable devices that send out a distress signal when manually activated or triggered by water immersion/sinking. A signal is picked up by satellites and relayed to maritime rescue authorities.

factory deck   the level below the main deck, just above water-line; almost enclosed, except for hatches and scuppers. On the *Sudur Havid* the factory deck held freezers, factory, crew cabins, galley and the crew mess.

freezer suit   an insulated, non-waterproof and quilted suit worn under waterproofs. Made from fibre insulation with a polyester shell fabric.

galley   the kitchen of a boat.

gantry   a metal arch structure used to lift objects and support pulleys for fishing operations.

GRT   gross register tonnage, a measure of the volume of permanently enclosed spaces in a ship. Not weight or displacement, but useful for comparing ships. Now generally referred to as gross tonnage.

hold   the storage area for cargo. On the *Sudur Havid* this held bait and catch, and was refrigerated to $-18\,^{\circ}$C.

hull   the entire hollow body of a ship, floating partly submerged in water. From the deck down the sides to the keel of the boat, but excludes superstructure.

immersion suit/survival suit   neoprene or fabric suit, donned in an emergency, which seals out water and keeps the wearer dry.

Inmarsat   the operators of a satellite system for maritime communications and safety.

keel   a beam that acts as the structural spine of the boat, along its bottom, from bow to stern.

knot   a speed of one nautical mile per hour (1.151 mph or 1.852 kmh).

leeward   the direction facing away from the wind (downwind).

life-raft   an inflatable rubber raft with canvas canopy, stored uninflated in a canister on deck. Provides an emergency refuge.

lightship weight   the weight of the ship with no cargo, fuel, crew or supplies aboard.

lower deck   the lowest level of the boat, below sea level. On the *Sudur Havid* this held the engine room, hold, crew cabins and tanks for oil, fuel and water.

main deck   the uppermost complete deck from bow to stern. On the *Sudur Havid* this held: the mast and derrick, winches, superstructure, rope crates and stern gantry.

Mess   the canteen or dining area.

nautical mile   a distance of 1.151 miles or 1.852 kilometres.

painter   a rope, usually attached to the bow, used for tying up or towing.

pitching   when the bow of the boat moves up and down

port to the left of the ship, when facing forward.

Rigid Raider small, fast fibreglass boats used by the armed forces for inshore operations.

SART Search and Rescue Transponder. A self-contained, waterproof device that emits a signal when detecting radar in use nearby, allowing a location to be determined.

scuppers slots cut through the hull of a boat, to allow water to drain from a deck.

snood the short length of line that attaches each hook to the rope fishing line.

Southern Ocean the name given by mariners to the waters surrounding Antarctica, formed by the southernmost portions of the Atlantic, Pacific and Indian oceans.

splicing the joining of pieces of rope by weaving their strands together, rather than by tying a knot.

stern the back end of the ship.

starboard to the right side of the ship, when facing forward.

storm door waterproof metal doors that seal the compartments of a boat, usually fastened by dogs.

superstructure the parts of the boat above the hull, projecting above the main deck. On the *Sudur Havid* the engine casing, Officers' Mess and cabins, and bridge.

tender a small boat used to ferry people or small goods between ships or to shore.

trawler a fishing boat that tows its net through the water.

treadplate a metal sheet with raised pattern for grip.

wheelhouse the structure housing the ship's wheel and other controls. Also called the bridge.

windward the direction facing into the wind (upwind).

BOAT PLANS AND MAPS

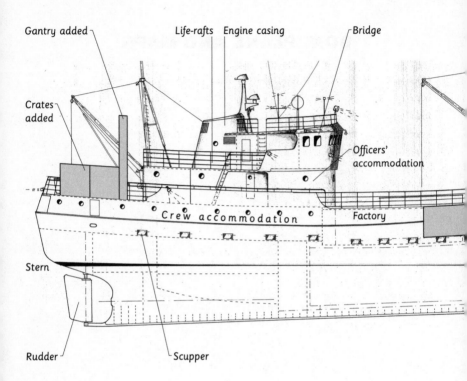

Gantry added — Life-rafts — Engine casing — Bridge

Crates added

Officers' accommodation

Crew accommodation — Factory

Stern

Rudder — Scupper

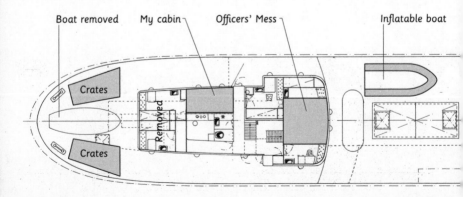

Boat removed — My cabin — Officers' Mess — Inflatable boat

Crates

Removed

Crates

Main deck

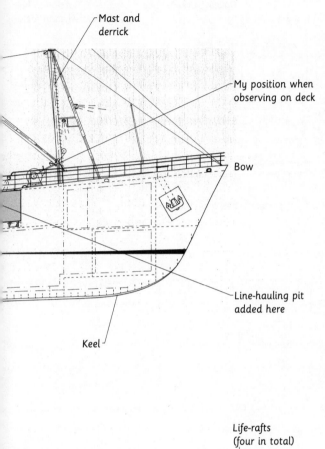

Mast and
derrick

My position when
observing on deck

Bow

Line-hauling pit
added here

Keel

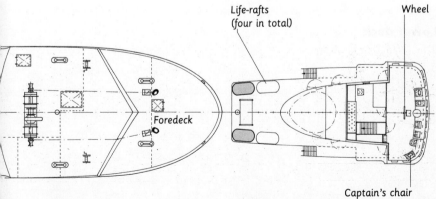

Life-rafts
(four in total)

Wheel

Foredeck

Captain's chair

Bridge

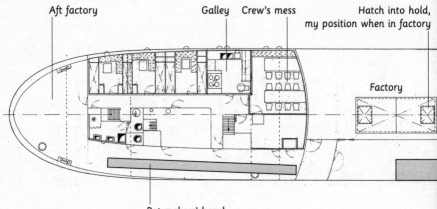

Aft factory   Galley   Crew's mess   Hatch into hold,
my position when in factory

Factory

Factory deck

Pot-makers' bench

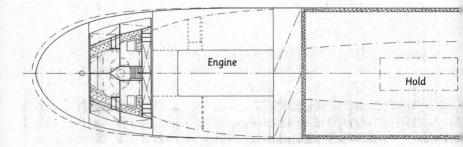

Engine

Hold

Lower deck

Taken from original 1963 yard drawings,
with relevant modifications marked

Freezer

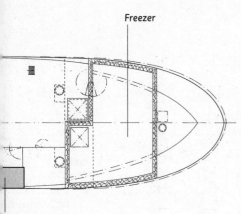

Line-hauling pit

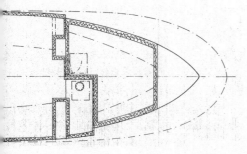

Vessel name:	*Sudur Havid*
Year of launch:	1964
Length:	44.70 metres
Breadth:	8.00 metres
Weight (unladen):	442.6 tonnes
GRT:	364 tonnes
Crew:	37 + 1 observer
Flag:	Republic of South Africa
Hold capacity:	310 metres^3
Engine power:	1200 horsepower
Fishing method:	Long-lining
Target species:	Patagonian toothfish

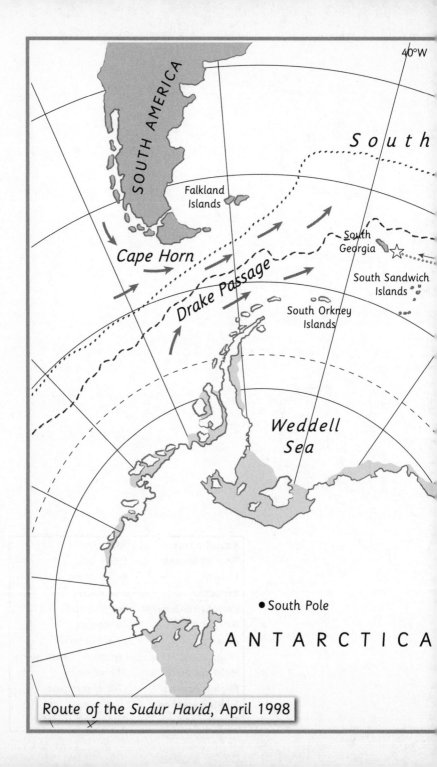

Route of the *Sudur Havid*, April 1998

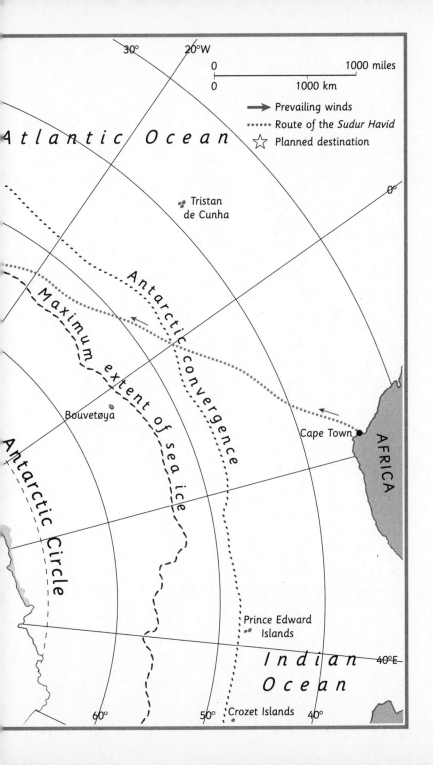

PROLOGUE

I'm waist-deep in seawater one degree below zero. My legs are numb, my fingers are frigid, and I cling to the inflatable arch which supports the roof of the flooded life-raft.

In the dim amber light I can just make out a few shapes around me. Bubbles, our Captain, lies slumped in the water, his head supported by his lifejacket. This is the same man who sang 'Flower of Scotland' over the radio to the Harbour Master each week as we reported our catches. He has a wife and kids back in Cape Town. Now he is barely alive, his chunky-knit jumper and tracksuit bottoms no match for the water, the hypothermia and the heart attack he suffered as we abandoned the boat.

Above us, the thin canvas canopy is our only shelter from the shrieking wind and the leviathan swells of the Southern Ocean. Every few minutes, the canopy is crushed against us by the crest of a breaking wave, flexing the inflatable life-raft as if folding it in two, jolting us from our contemplations.

Slowly, I sing to myself, 'Will your anchor hold in the storms of life . . .' They are lines from my favourite song from Sunday school. I don't have a single drop of maritime blood in my body, so Heaven knows why I liked the song when I was a child, but it seems fitting now.

God, if I survive this . . .

What? What am I willing to promise to be out of this situation? I change my prayer.

God, help me to survive this.

*

I

There is little human noise. Any talk of rescue has long died away, and those who were wailing have stopped. Each person has sunk into his own struggle to survive. In the darkness, Big Danie pulls Morné and Eugene close, trying to keep them warm. Morné can feel Danie's giant hands shaking.

Suddenly Bubbles' voice cuts across the raft, roll-calling each of the crew he can remember. Seventeen of us boarded the raft.

'Morné?'

'Yes, Skipper.'

'Brian?'

'Yes, Skipper.'

'Matt?'

'Yeah, I'm OK, I'm here.'

The roll-call goes on. It serves as a call to attention, making each of us respond, and a brief reminder that we are not alone. But it also brings events into stark definition. Although my mind is clouded by the cold, I am sure there were more people on the raft than Bubbles is calling out now, and some no longer answer.

Beneath me, weak orbs of silver light glow up from the water. The fading bulbs are attached to lifejackets, which are attached to bodies. I can feel limbs and objects under my feet and knees and sense that they are not alive. I cannot bring myself to care as long as they offer some support to keep me above the chill of the water.

Boetie has been acting strangely since his head was battered by the steel hull of the boat when we abandoned ship. Tonnes of pressure versus one human skull? No contest, even if the skull is South African. Bubbles ends his latest roll-call by shouting out for his best friend.

'Boetie?'

No reply.

'Boetie? . . . Boetie?'

'He is dead, man,' said Hannes. 'Stop.'

ONE

ESCAPE

1

DEPARTURE

Wednesday, 1 April 1998

The woman on the phone, Louise, was cordial but brief. The fishing boat, now waiting in Cape Town, would sail 3,000 miles down to sub-Antarctic South Georgia. If I took the position, I would be working as a Scientific Observer on the Southern Ocean for the next three months. I knew little of the reality I was to face: icebergs, killer whales and ocean swells as high as houses, not to mention some of the wildest weather in the world.

I had been looking for a job in marine biology after completing a Master's degree at Aberdeen. Opportunities had sprung up and snapped away my course-mates, taking them off to new and exciting positions around the world. For me, a few months' work at the university was followed by a disappointing few weeks on the dole; I was working as an office porter just to keep my pride up. Four years of study, so many dreams of aquatic adventure, and now I was stuck trolleying paper around the photocopiers in an Aberdeen office block.

All I needed was some 'experience', that all-important kick-start to get my professional life moving. During a chance conversation, a friend from the Zoology department reminded me that he had worked for a short while aboard fishing boats around the Falkland Islands. The job sounded tough but rewarding and he scribbled down the address of a consultancy group in London who recruited such scientists. Several weeks and phone conversations passed until late on a Wednesday afternoon, on 1 April, a message came through on my pager to 'Call Louise'. The deployment she was offering me started in just two days. Surely this was the break I needed; the adventure I craved.

Friday, 3 April 1998

Corinne gave me a lift to Aberdeen Airport in her old blue Fiat for the red-eye flight to London. She was happily chatting about the trip and what we would do on my return, and we seemed to fit a month's conversation into the short journey.

We had met through the university SCUBA diving club and had been seeing each other for just over a year, living together for the past few months. She had seen my frustrations grow and she was excited and supportive that I had a chance to prove myself.

We were prepared for a swift separation, but this was much quicker than either of us anticipated. I would be away at least three months, possibly longer, maybe out of contact for the entire time. I began to feel anxious. The Southern Ocean is a hostile place and I was unsure of the welcome I would receive aboard the boat, as a university upstart recording the conduct of hardened fishermen.

The night before, in our room, I had bundled the few possessions from the kit-list into a rucksack: thick thermals, thick jumpers and thick books. This may have been my first time as an Observer, and my first trip to the Southern Ocean, but I had spent a few weeks on yachts and research vessels. This was long enough to know that warm clothes and a few good tomes were part of an essential high-seas survival kit.

At the gate through to security we kissed goodbye. I could see tears in her eyes, and her lips trembled as she told me I'd be fine.

'I'll see you in a few months,' I promised. 'The time will fly by.'

Watching her blonde curls and brown padded jacket disappear into the crowd, I headed through to my flight.

*

By lunchtime I was climbing the steps to an impressive Georgian building in Kensington, just in time for my departure briefing. Louise greeted me in the hall, and led me through to the far less impressive and drab company offices. She was young and bubbly, and I relaxed a little. In the stuffy reception area she introduced me to another new Observer, Magnus Johnson. Lanky and friendly, with short dark hair and a heavy brow, Magnus was a few years older than me. His name and soft Shetland timbre gave away his roots, but for the last few years he had been studying in Leicester for a doctorate.

Together we were run through our roles and responsibilities. We were to be stationed on two long-lining vessels shortly to set sail from Cape Town for the Southern Ocean. Once aboard, we would observe the boats' fishing operations, reporting our findings to the company on our return to the UK. Our main tasks would include counting and measuring catch, recording compliance with international fishing regulations and, perhaps most importantly, watching for endangered albatrosses that had accidentally been caught.

Eager to prove ourselves, Magnus and I listened intently and made notes. Despite the overflowing lever-arch files of instructions and protocol that sat on the desks in front of us, we scribbled as though we were competing with each other.

At the end of the briefing, after we had filled in the paperwork, the last task was vessel allocation. Louise thrust a printed spreadsheet across the table towards us.

'So, which boat do you want to go on?' she asked, glancing at us. 'We need to decide now, for contact details.'

The two boats were the *Northern Pride* and the *Sudur Havid*, its foreign name an awkward and unfamiliar blend of syllables. Our tongues tripped over the pronunciation. *Soo-dur Have-id*. Magnus and I looked at each other and shrugged. The names of the boats meant nothing to us at this point.

We were given some more basic information. Both vessels were Cape Town registered, and owned by the same company, but the *Northern Pride* had Spanish officers, which probably meant Spanish speakers, while the *Sudur Havid*'s were South Africans, who would be more likely to speak English. I kept quiet, not wanting to say that I couldn't be bothered to learn a language. The voyage would be difficult enough.

We could have flipped a coin, or drawn straws. I waited for Magnus to express an opinion.

After just a few seconds, he declared, 'Oh well, I quite fancy learning Spanish.'

'I don't,' I responded, adding quickly, 'I'll take the *Sudur Havid*.'

It seemed so easy and unimportant a choice at the time, sitting in a comfortable London office. Then again, some of life's most pivotal decisions seem that way when they are made. Magnus would be aboard the *Northern Pride*; I would live and work on the *Sudur Havid*, call sign ZU1047: Zulu Uniform One Zero Four Seven. The name may have been foreign to me, but in the language of her first home, the Faroe Islands, it means *Southern Ocean*.

We were to fly to Cape Town the same day, at 19:00. The vessel owners were keen to get moving. The fishery had already opened for the season two days earlier, on 1 April, but the boats were not allowed to fish without an Observer. The owners had been slow to organize their fishing licences, which cost £60,000 for each boat, and the departure had been further delayed because the *Sudur Havid* was awaiting the issue of a safety certificate. Although the fishing season ran until the end of August, it would be cut short if the quota for the whole fishery was reached. The first week of the season was famous for particularly good catches, and rival crews were already on-site, hauling in the prize: Patagonian toothfish. Once out of port, it would still take us two weeks to join them. Expensive time was ticking.

Briefing finished, we rooted around the office basement frantically scavenging and packing oilskins, rubber gloves, knives and measuring boards. A one-piece blue and red deck-suit, waterproof with buoyant insulation, looked practical and warm. Being someone on the small side of average – 5′8″, eleven stone, and size eight shoes – my clothing was relatively easy to source, except for a deck lifejacket. For some reason, there were none of these available. For 6′4″ Magnus, there seemed to be nothing left in the right size. We were the last Observers to be deployed on the fishery for the season, and most of the kit had already been issued. Given that we were expected to work on deck in all conditions, the omissions were troubling. We both at least expected to have the right equipment.

London sped by outside the taxi windows as Magnus and I hurtled towards Heathrow Airport, late for our flight. Rucksacks and canvas army kitbags washed from side to side on the floor of the black cab. An omen, perhaps.

£500 lighter after paying British Airways the excess baggage, we passed through to duty-free and stocked up on our final essentials. Magnus sought out a huge pack of noxiously strong Gauloises cigarettes; I bought a couple of extra books. Nicotine and words to take the edge off the long voyage ahead of us.

We drank beer and chatted at one of the expensive seafood bars that pepper Heathrow's terminals. In glass cabinets, mussels and oysters lay clenched in their shells on gleaming ice. They piqued my interest as a biologist, but not my appetite. I was starting to feel apprehensive and inadequate. Magnus had worked on a number of British and Russian research ships as part of his PhD studies; my CV paled in comparison.

We boarded our flight and settled in for the long overnight haul to Cape Town. The dense files of regulations were awkward to fit on the tiny aeroplane tables, but we wanted to familiarize ourselves with the job at hand before we met our crews. Magnus read aloud from the section covering life on the boat.

'Observers are expected to dress appropriately for meals in the Officers' Mess.'

It conjured up images of brandy and evening dress at the Captain's Table on an ocean liner, of polite conversation and epaulettes. We were to have an officer's privileges on the boat, which meant better accommodation, food and conditions than the rest of the crew, but not an officer's responsibilities. We were not expected to have any role in the daily running of the vessels, which was perfectly fine by me.

I was more interested in the wildlife than the protocol. Despite the poorly printed black-and-white pictures in the identification guide, which were uninspiring and largely unhelpful, I couldn't wait to see the weird and wonderful deep-sea fishes, killer whales, sperm whales, albatrosses and fur seals. I was to be paid to watch species I had dreamed about, in one of the world's wildest places. Whatever lay ahead, the journey was underway, and I fell uneasily to sleep in my seat.

2

ALL ABOARD

Saturday, 4 April 1998

Three days had passed since I last filled a photocopier with paper, and work was now much more to my liking. At the bustling airport arrivals gate, a waiting driver with a sign met us and took our trolley, stacked with bags. Though it was early in the day, the dry warmth of Cape Town hit us as we stepped out of the building. The driver whisked us straight off to a dusty white minibus. The clock really was ticking. He was to take us directly down to the docks.

I had travelled to Zambia, Tanzania and Kenya in the decade before and had observed first-hand the faded colonial infrastructure. The smooth roads and flyovers of Cape Town were a world apart. Stylish glass office buildings and sports grounds whizzed past the minibus windows and large houses with neat lawns were surrounded by exuberant pink and orange flowers. The sunshine and vivid colours were glorious after dismal Aberdeen. I wanted to stay and explore; it seemed a shame to arrive in such a beautiful place and then leave so quickly; but we were here for a job. The minibus pulled in through the security gates of the port, and drove slowly along the broad industrial quays past an assortment of cargo ships and cranes.

When the bus came to a halt on the dockside, Magnus and I jumped out, eager to see the boats that we would be working on. Two men waiting in smart trousers and open-necked shirts came over to greet us. I was particularly aware of the need to act professionally. I was twenty-three years old, though I probably looked even younger, and didn't have the sort of appearance that commanded respect: short, skinny and scruffy. If I was to be a good Observer, and to practise the skills and knowledge I learned at university, I would need to be taken seriously.

'Welcome to South Africa, gentlemen. I see you've left the British weather at home. My name's Alan Newman, I'm the vessel manager.'

Alan's warm handshake let us relax for a moment. Short, round and bearded, he asked a few questions about our journey before introducing us to his younger colleague.

'This is Sean Walker, he's here representing the owners.'

Sean had his long brown hair pulled back in a ponytail, like mine. At sea, we were to have minimal contact with Alan and Sean – they were office men, after all – but we needed to make a good impression to ensure amicable relations on the boat. We had been warned that Observers were often resented. It was a condition of the vessel's fishing licence that an Observer had to be carried, but this did not mean that we would be welcomed. Who would want someone watching over their shoulder as they work? Both Alan and Sean were polite and business-like, but they were clearly in a hurry to get the boats to sea.

We walked away from the minibus, towards the boats tied alongside the concrete quay. A blue and white bow loomed high above our heads. The *Northern Pride* sat proud of the dock, projecting the sort of dependability you could believe would punch through the giant fifteen-metre-high swells of the Southern Ocean. A strong steel gantry towered on her deck, pure white against the blue sky, festooned with marine electronics, pulleys and lights. With a fresh coat of blue paint on her fifty-metre hull, the *Pride* was substantial and impressive.

And behind her? What was that grubby little boat? The small dark-blue one, with a bit more rust and missing the gleam. A sequence of thoughts rattled through my head.

Oh my God, that's the Sudur Havid. *That's the boat I'm living on for the next three months. Is it too late to change my mind?*

Her heavily built steel hull sat low in the water and was short and stout. At forty-five metres in length she was bigger than the fishing boats in most English harbours, but smaller than many Scottish super-trawlers I had seen in ports around my home in Aberdeen. Functional rather than elegant, she should have seemed marginally shorter than the *Pride*, but she was dwarfed. Far back on her pea-green deck, the windows of her white wheelhouse barely peeped over her rust-pocked bow. From the wheelhouse the Skipper and officers could control the ship and watch the seas ahead; two thirds of the boat was in front of them in the form of an open, unsheltered deck. There was only a small deck behind that towards the stern, which was crowded with wooden crates and steel gantries. A gaping hole in the side of the boat was level with the dock, and I could see rollers and winches attached inside. That, I reasoned, must be where the fishing line came on board. A row of buoys sat atop her wheelhouse structure, just above the windows, like neon orange and pink eyebrows. The comical sight of a boat with a face did little to make me trust her more.

I made the mistake of helping Magnus aboard the *Northern Pride* with his kit and saw the wide passages and his spacious, pleasant personal cabin. Alan Newman then led me back to the *Sudur Havid* and we climbed aboard for a quick tour. Returning the favour, Magnus was quiet as we ricocheted along the narrow, poorly lit corridors like rats along a drainpipe, and struggled to get my huge kitbags into the tiny cabin I was to share with Glen Petersen, an engineer. Our cabin was typical: one small bunk each (Glen on top bunk, me on the bottom) opposite the single porthole, one drawer each underneath the bunks for storage, one cupboard each for clothes and kit, and a small padded bench by the door. Glen came in, and politely introduced himself. Old and wizened, with rich-coloured skin and wiry hair, he was fastidiously neat. His reading glasses were clipped to his chest pocket and his clothes were folded and stowed. His bunk was already carefully made, folded just so. Everything else inside the room was made of varnished plywood or melamine, yellowed with age and wear. A stale odour hung in the cabin, of fried food, diesel and tobacco smoke. Under my breath, I cursed my casual choice of boat back in London. This was just typical of my luck. Still, Magnus may have got the better deal on boats, but what about the officers and crew?

Baggage stowed, Alan led us off for the official introductions. He called in Afrikaans to a man climbing the steep steps to the bridge. Filling the width of the stairs, Bubbles was as wide as an ape. In fact, if you took a pair of hair clippers to a sleeping gorilla, you wouldn't be too far off producing a good likeness. He turned when Alan called but it was hard at first to make out his features in the murky light. Stepping back down the stairway he rolled from side to side towards us along the corridor. It was apparent now that he was as short as he was wide, with rough white skin and a dark beard. A pair of luminous sapphire eyes peered out from the small gap above his beard and below his thick-set brow. Eventually, a smile erupted.

'Newman, you Jewish bastard, how's it?'

Alan laughed off the insult and carried on.

'Matt, this is Bubbles. He'll be your Skipper.'

Gerard McDonagh was always referred to by his nickname, Bubbles. His gruff demeanour and scowl as we met made it seem all the more absurd. This was further compounded by his striking resemblance to the white supremacist Eugene Terre'Blanche. This was the man I would be trusting with my life. I wondered if Magnus hadn't got the better deal with officers, too.

Alan led me up the steep stairs to the bridge, where he introduced me to Boetie, the Fishing Master. Like Bubbles, he was never referred to by his real name – Brian – rather as Boetie, *little brother*. Whereas Bubbles would navigate us towards the fishing grounds, Boetie would be in charge of the boat as soon as the fishing line hit the water. Tall, solidly built and possessed of a healthy tan, Boetie grinned as he greeted me, although I had the unnerving feeling that I was being assessed.

'How's it, Matt?'

His small moustache emphasized the neatly clipped way in which he spoke, which was slightly squeaky and unexpected in someone so large. It was a complete contrast to Bubbles' rumblings.

Both men were proud of the racial make-up of the thirty-seven-strong crew. As far as they knew, we were the first boat out of Cape Town to consist of a fully integrated team of 'whites, blacks and coloureds'.

They told me that the white South Africans on the *Sudur Havid*, from Skipper to deckhand, came from a variety of backgrounds, including the city, the coast and the farms.

'Do you speak any Afrikaans?' Bubbles asked me.

'Not a word. Do I need to?'

'No, you'll be fine,' he said dismissively. 'Most of the South African guys speak English. We'll teach you a bit as we go along.'

The black crew were predominantly either Xhosa from South Africa or Ovambo from Namibia. Some of the Namibians had been fishing for years, and had served on the *Sudur Havid* when she previously worked out of Walvis Bay, Namibia. Others had only recently come down to South Africa in search of better-paid work. As well as their own tribal languages, on the boat the Ovambo spoke mainly Portuguese. Just a few spoke Afrikaans or English.

I wasn't familiar with the group termed 'Cape Coloureds'. Regardless of their ancestry – mixed race or Cape Bushmen, Indian or Malay – these men were classed as 'coloured' because their skin was brown or honey-toned and not black or white. Most of them had grown up in and around Cape Town, and their names were more familiar to me than those of the Xhosa or Ovambo:

Brian, Trevor and Gideon were Cape Coloured; Walu Walu and Kashingola were not.

In total, about a third of the ship's complement was Cape Coloured, a third was black and a third was white, including officers from Portugal, Germany and, with my arrival, the UK.

Magnus and I climbed ashore and followed Alan to the comfortable saloon of the *Northern Pride*, where we gathered around the tables on the cushioned benches for an officers' meeting. Magnus and I were wary. We were new at the job and didn't want to appear naive. If we were not careful, we could lose our objectivity and become puppets to the Skippers. I stifled any nervous jokes during the meeting and shook hands as firmly as I could when they were offered.

Looking around the table, I saw the people I would soon hear as voices from the radio or see as names on faxes. The Captain of the *Northern Pride*, Andreas, seemed much more affable than Bubbles, and was enthusiastic about the trip ahead. Sean, Alan and the other company men began their pitch, keen to assure us that they really cared about the boats' conduct. They were clear in asking the Skippers and Fishing Masters to treat us courteously and to adhere to the fishery regulations.

We left the crew of the *Northern Pride* to prepare for departure and chatted on the dock. Magnus puffed nervously on one of his cigarettes, delaying boarding the *Pride* until the very last moment. We shook hands, and I wished him a safe trip. Calm seas beckoned, and the *Northern Pride* sailed out of Cape Town at 16:20. The dock was now almost empty of people. Alan raised his hand in a final salute to Captain Andreas. He clearly had similar thoughts to mine about the *Pride* as we watched the big blue boat glide across the harbour.

'She's a beautiful boat, eh?'

The *Sudur Havid*, still tied to the harbourside, had none of her sister's grace, but looking at her now on her own she didn't seem quite as small, or quite as ugly, no longer overshadowed by the *Northern Pride*. In any case, it was now too late to swap.

3

ANATOMY OF THE *SUDUR HAVID*

It seemed strange that two boats could not be fuelled on the same day, but that was the reason I was given for a two-day delay in our departure. With time to kill, I made an effort to familiarize myself with my new home.

It didn't take long to explore the *Sudur Havid*. She was only small, and felt smaller still: her navy-blue hull was 44.7 metres long overall, from the tip of her stumpy dented bow to the butt of her rusty stern ramp, and about eight metres wide. In terms of weight she was about 440 tonnes unladen, with a Gross Register Tonnage of 364 tonnes. To put it another way, she was just a little longer than the biggest blue whale, but four times heavier. Not a big space to fit thirty-eight men and their work and lives into for months at a time.

I doubted that she had ever been elegant, but guessed that she was once the pearl of her owner's eye. Built in Norway in 1964, originally as a trawler, her first home port was Torshavn in the Faroe Islands. For twenty years she safely carried a complement of twenty-seven men as far north as Greenland and across to the rich grounds of Newfoundland. Over the years she had been modified as different fishing techniques were used. She still bore the remnants of a stern ramp, once used for hauling in nets and prawns, which cut through her transom. Now redundant, it was obscured by the changes and additions required for her new life as a long-liner.

Below the waterline, her hull was taken up with the hold for the catch, fuel and water tanks, as well as a few cabins for the crew and the engine room. The last of our food was being loaded into the hold. This was a giant freezer, divided up into bays by planks to keep bait, catch and food separate, and to ensure that the boat remained stable when the weather was rough. It was stacked high with hundreds of boxes of bait, ready for the trip ahead. With any luck, in a few months' time these boxes of cheap sardines and horse mackerel would be replaced by sacks of frozen toothfish.

The unluckiest crew members were stuck in two stifling cabins directly behind the engine room. Just millimetres of steel separated the occupants of these tiny underwater cells from the engine and the sea, and the cabins were filled with the constant din of the engines and the wash of the water around the hull.

The engine room, accessed down a steep flight of metal stairs, would be deafeningly loud when at full throttle, but at least it was warm and clean. The huge 1200-horsepower engine sat like a queen ant being tended by her diligent workers. This was the realm of Klaus, Glen and the other engineers and was strictly off-limits to 90 per cent of the crew. My cabin-mate, Glen, served resentfully as Klaus's deputy. Although both were qualified as Chief Engineers, Glen had been temporarily reassigned to the *Sudur Havid* from another boat and had taken on a Second Engineer's role. Strict shift working would mean that they could keep out of each other's way once we departed.

Glen and Klaus were new to the boat, but each had decades of experience. They were assisted and towered over by Alfius, a Second Engineer by qualification but aboard now as a Greaser – an engine room skivvy. Tall, dark-skinned and bearded, the Namibian was a physically impressive figure but stuttered nervously as he talked. His anxiety clashed with their quiet routines. Although he was supposed to be familiar with the boat, and had worked on it before, Glen and Klaus seemed to think that they could keep it running more smoothly without his bumbling help.

Melvin, whom I briefly saw running around with a screwdriver, was the ship's electrician. By the time we eventually reached the Southern Ocean they would be joined by Little Danie, who had come aboard recovering from a fractured ankle, just out of a plaster cast. The cold decks of the factory would cause him too much pain so he was reassigned to be a Greaser, where the warmth of the engine room better suited his ankle and his general allergy to work.

Moving up a deck to the waterline, the lower deck of the boat held the factory, blast freezers, the galley and the crew's quarters. The factory took up the largest part of this level, about twelve metres long and the whole eight-metre width of the boat. The exposed steelwork of the vessel had been painted white and lines of fluorescent lights hung above the various stainless steel benches and tubs, which were to be used to head, gut and clean the fish. Chutes brought the fish into the factory on the starboard side, and they would then be passed clockwise around the factory before ending up in the freezers towards the bow.

A door on the starboard side of the factory led out to a small 'balcony' area which was known as the line-hauling pit. Here, the side of the ship had been cut away, and a newer metal wall had been installed a metre further inboard, to allow the hooks and fishing line to be brought in closer to sea level. This modified platform would be exposed to the worst of the elements and the waves, and gave limited protection to the operator of the line hauler winch.

Further back, the factory narrowed to a corridor, along which ran rusty steel benches where the pots of hooks would be baited and readied. At the stern of the boat, the factory widened again to form a preparation area, with a hatch from which the hooks and line were put into the water again. Squeezed into the small amount of space left to the port of the vessel, between the forward and aft sections of the working factory area, were the galley and crew quarters.

The tiny galley was empty and quiet. A massive pan swayed on its gimbal frame as the boat rolled gently. I couldn't believe that such a tiny space would be used to produce all our meals, but at least it looked hygienic. The tired melamine surfaces and tiled walls were scrubbed clean.

I stuck my head into one of the cabins for the deck and factory crew. It was cramped and scruffy, fitted with triple-deck bunks piled with clothes waiting to be stowed. There were eight beds in the tiny room, and barely space for two men to stand, let alone dress. It felt wrong to step over the threshold so I continued, nearing the end of my exploration.

I made my way up the stairs, and out on to the main deck. Most of the boat at this level was exposed to the elements, and the floor was painted bright green and rimmed by white railings. Anything steel, and almost everything outside the boat was made from steel, was rough and pitted with decades of rust, wear and layers of paint. Cold to the touch, all was covered with a film of salt.

The centre of the deck was home to the winches used to haul in the fishing line, and a white mast towered over it supporting a derrick (or hoist) to lift the boxes in and out of the hold. There was also a small, pale-grey inflatable boat, known as the 'rubber duck'. This would be used as a tender, to carry people and supplies to shore or between boats.

Behind the wheelhouse, the small stern deck was dominated by two rows of giant wood and metal crates which had been added to hold the fishing lines. A narrow alleyway ran through them. The boat carried two complete lines, plus spares and anchor lines. In total, this measured at least sixty kilometres of 20mm-thick rope.

Making my way back inside the superstructure on the main deck, I found the Officers' Mess and quarters, where I shared my cabin with Glen. This area consisted of four cabins which were bigger and less crowded than those of the crew, and also possessed the luxury of a toilet and shower exclusively for us. However, this wasn't as glamorous as it sounded and only meant that eight men were now politely sharing a cold, draughty metal cupboard, rather than thirty.

Magnus and I had guessed that the *Sudur Havid* was not the sort of boat to have a Captain's Table, bedecked with fine china and glassware. Instead, the Officers' Mess was a small, snug room – no more than three by two metres – lined with plywood. A vinyl-cushioned bench wrapping around the three sides of a central table was enough seating for six or seven at a squeeze. There was no heating. A small fridge was screwed to the wall, and a TV on a shelf high up in one corner completed an already cluttered room.

Lastly, above the main deck, in the highest level of the superstructure, was the bridge. This would be the nerve centre of the boat. The work may go on downstairs, but the decisions would be made up here. Its many windows offered a sweeping view of the conditions ahead and the working deck below, and it was home to all of the burbling radios and navigation equipment, as well as the ship's wheel and engine controls. The paint on the steel wheel was chipped although the wheel was almost redundant now. The *Sudur Havid* was controlled instead by the autopilot or a small lever beside the Captain's chair to starboard.

A small cabin which led off from the bridge, once the navigation room, was used by Bubbles and Boetie. The bridge itself was accessed by a very steep and narrow staircase, though I was told that Bubbles and Boetie used it as rarely as possible, preferring to stand at the top and yell 'Simon-ye!', if they needed Simon, the Steward, to bring them a coffee.

The bridge was set apart from the process of fishing and would be clean, dry and warm, not to mention fish-free. Bubbles and Boetie could observe and command the daily lives of their crew from the safety and comfort of this watchtower that gazed down upon the main deck. In terms of dress, both Bubbles and Boetie shunned oilskin fishing wear for jogging bottoms and a sweatshirt.

Boetie finished his ensemble off with beige suede safari boots and a thin blue golfing jacket. Bubbles, meanwhile, was wearing thick socks and sandals. Hardly appropriate deck wear, but then Bubbles would never be on deck.

'How's it, Engelsman?' Boetie asked, catching my glance.

'Not bad. *Lekker* [good], I should say,' I replied, trying out my Afrikaans. 'I was just wondering. What's a Hottentot?'

Klaus had been muttering loudly about certain Cape Coloured members of the crew being 'Fucking Hottentots'. Without an encyclopedia, and to break the ice, I decided to ask the Fishing Master.

'Hottentots is not a nice word, Matt. It was old slang for the Bushmen, and some people used it for all the coloureds,' he answered. 'And make sure you don't call people Kaffirs either. That's the black guys. Not a polite term.'

Boetie explained that along with some of the other white crew on board, he had served in the South African armed forces. This was during the same period that some of the Ovambo men on the boat could have been fighting against them for Namibian independence.

'You know, a few years ago we might have been shooting at each other. But here we are working and living on a boat together. What a turnaround, eh? The old racist types always make out the Cape Coloureds to be thieves, as though they couldn't work. You watch on this boat and see if they can work.'

4

THE PAPER CAPTAIN

10:00, Monday, 6 April 1998

Unbeknownst to me, we had been waiting for another crew member, who was flying in from Iceland. This was the real reason for the delay in departure, not fuel. Bjorgvin Armannsson was startlingly pale and tall as he climbed stiffly up from the quay on to the boat. Well over six feet, his height made awkward by a slight stoop, he looked to be about sixty years old but still had a full mop of dark-brown hair, flopped over to one side of his head in a parting.

Bubbles explained to me that Bjorgvin had been hired by the vessel operators to have his Captain's certificate aboard, rather than his skills. While Bubbles and Boetie had been in command when the boat sailed out of Namibia, neither held the level of qualification that would allow them to captain a South African fishing vessel in a high-seas zone; the company had been forced to hire someone who was certified. According to Bubbles, he and Boetie would still be in charge; Bjorgvin was to be our 'Paper Captain'.

Bubbles led him to his cabin, and quickly got him settled into his place on the boat.

'Think of it as a holiday, Bjorgvin.'

'But I won't get paid!'

'You will. Just make sure you don't get under Boetie's feet once we're fishing.'

'I will need something . . . to do.'

A long pause interrupted Bjorgvin's song-like Scandinavian speech as he struggled to find the correct words in English.

To keep him placated, Bjorgvin was assigned the night watch. He would stay awake in the wheelhouse to check the boat's course, the radar screen and the sea conditions while the other officers slept. He had spent twenty years of his working life at sea around Iceland, mostly on trawlers, in some of the roughest, coldest waters of the North Atlantic. In the last few years he had worked ashore variously as a police officer, a mental nurse and a fur farmer, but he had tired of these 'mundane' land jobs. In need of money, Bjorgvin was back at sea. Night watch wasn't quite the stimulating return he had expected, but it was a start.

Bjorgvin's 'arrangement' did little to settle my nerves. The initial excitement and inertia of the trip was fading fast and, with Magnus already miles out at sea, I was getting cold feet. I spurred myself into getting organized on board and meeting more new people. An enormous young white guy was leaning against the railing of the boat, smoking. He had cropped blond hair with a thin moustache, and his hands were almost as big as my head. *Christ, he looks intimidating*, I thought, and decided I would introduce myself to someone else, first. He didn't speak as I walked past.

Waiting for me on my bunk was a crate of beer and a freezer suit, which was essentially a thick quilted waistcoat and trousers to be worn under my oilskins. It was not expensive or stylish but functional. Hearing that I'd been sent from home without one, Boetie had kindly ordered it for me especially.

I left my cabin to find and thank him, but the corridor was blocked by the enormous young guy from the railing, who was trying to show Boetie a problem with his own freezer suit.

'Danie, don't be ridiculous, there can't be that much of a differ-ence between XXL and XXXL.'

'But, Skipper, look!'

Danie struggled into the XXL jacket but there was a six-inch gap between the sides of the zips.

'OK, Danie, I take your point, I'll see if we can get XXXL before we leave.'

At 15:00 we finally departed, with thirty-eight people aboard. The first Monday in April is said to be an inauspicious day to set sail as it was the day that Cain slew Abel, but I was just anxious to find out what life on the voyage ahead would hold. For most of the crew, this was just another fishing trip, and they busied themselves tidying up and stowing the last of the stores. Now we were moving, the boat thrummed with the drone of the engine and the billowy, burbling exhalations of the exhausts. This was to be our soundtrack day and night, our constant companion for the voyage.

It was a sunny afternoon, and the breeze across the deck was pleasant, but the sea state had deteriorated in the two days since the *Northern Pride* had left. Long, slow swells rolled the boat as we sailed out of the shelter of the harbour breakwater, and my legs got used to balancing on a moving deck, a movement that would not stop for three months.

I had an empty, gnawing feeling in my stomach. I've never suffered from full-blown seasickness, but I was feeling a bit queasy. I knew that in a few days my body would return to normal, but right now some food would settle my stomach.

Grunter was Chief Cook of the small, sweltering kitchen. Here he would produce three meals a day for all thirty-eight aboard. Named for his large lips, which resembled the grunter fish, I was told that he always managed to stay calm and composed in his clean white apron, and was often to be heard singing a church hymn. I could sense that he was clearly a relaxed hand at sea when we were introduced.

Grunter reassured me. When I asked him about our journey ahead, he replied confidently.

'You know, Matt, I am a believer, and Jesus will keep us safe.'

Grunter wasn't alone in the kitchen. On this trip he had the bonus of his seventeen-year-old son, Gideon, to keep him company. Gideon was working as the Galley Boy, partly as a chance for Grunter to spend some time with the teenager. I met Grunter's other assistant, Simon, as he laid the table in the Officers' Mess. He told me he was from Namibia, as he slowly and deliberately placed each item of cutlery on the table. I hoped that he would speed up once we were working, otherwise mealtimes might take a while.

I grabbed a bread roll and some cheese and stood by the door looking out on to the deck, watching the view go by. Table Mountain, its iconic profile looming over Cape Town, stood moody against platinum cloud. Robben Island sat low against the seascape, uninviting and fringed by waves. Now vacated by its most famous inhabitant, it was barren and desolate. The food calmed my stomach, and gave it something to work on, but I was still apprehensive about the trip ahead and how I would fit in as the naive newcomer on such an established boat.

Adding to my unease was the fact that there had been no mention of safety. On aeroplanes you are given a briefing even if you are flying for just an hour, while on scientific trawlers in Scotland I had gone through abandon-ship drills, racing to muster stations and donning survival suits. I remembered how awkward and uncomfortable the neoprene survival suits had felt, but they completely sealed out the water and I appreciated that they were a crucial emergency aid. Now, with months at sea ahead in one of the most hostile areas of the world, I hadn't even been told where my lifejacket was kept.

I asked Glen, and he led me to a padlocked cupboard next to our toilet. This was where the lifejackets were stored but, to prevent the contents being stolen and sold, one of the officers, Joaquim, kept the only key.

Furthermore, there were no fully sealed survival suits on board, which in the event of an emergency would help keep a man alive submerged in freezing water. I had the blue and red deck-suit issued to me in London and the freezer suit from Boetie, but if I fell overboard these would be far less effective.

The life-rafts were hard to miss: four big white capsules sat in cradles just behind the bridge. I read the odd faded notices hanging on the wall of the crew's mess: 'abandon ship, boarding a life-raft, fighting fires at sea'. Bubbles and Boetie hadn't mentioned any actions I should take in an emergency, or drills. Being a novice, I assumed that this was the way things were done on a commercial fishing boat. They had been at sea so long, I reasoned, they must have done it all too many times before.

Back on the bridge, Bubbles was snoring on the small bench like a hibernating bear, but stirred when I came in. He rolled to his feet, and yelled down the stairs.

'Simon-ye! Coffee, if you please!'

Boetie was slouched in the high leather chair. It seemed like a good chance to chat, and I tried to break the ice and get to know them. I had seen *Titanic* with Leonardo DiCaprio and Kate Winslet just before I left for Cape Town.

'So, have you guys seen *Titanic* then? I thought it was pretty good. The sinking scene is amazing . . .'

I tailed off; they were both looking at me with faces like stone. Boetie let me know why.

'Matt, we don't talk about such things, not on board.'

We were only a day out of port when we had to turn around unexpectedly. Two pumps, normally hidden under grilles in the floor on either side of the factory, had burned out. These pumps were necessary to expel any water that had entered the factory deck through the hatches for the fish and the line. The hatches had to remain open when fishing, and could not be made completely watertight when closed. Furthermore, many of the scuppers in the factory, through which water could drain away, had been welded shut. Vital for the day-to-day safety of the boat, the pumps were now useless.

Unfazed by the severity of the problem, I reasoned that at least it meant another day or two before I would have to start work. The Skipper and vessel owners were more troubled by the delay. Desperate to get the boat turned around as soon as possible, they promised we would only be back in Cape Town for a few hours.

Thursday, 9 April 1998

When we tied up alongside the jetty, Klaus the Chief Engineer worked with Alan Newman and the company's land-based engineer to fit the replacement pumps. Glen busied himself fixing a leak in the bow fuel tank. Worryingly, it had already leaked diesel into the fish hold. If this happened with fish in the hold it would be a disaster, spoiling the catch and leaving it valueless. The boat was a hive of engineering activity as various problems were ironed out. I took the last chance to stretch my legs, and walked up and down the quay.

Klaus was one of the most senior officers aboard. On many boats the Chief Engineer is considered second only to the Skipper. Small and stocky, balding with greying hair, he wore a boiler suit, glasses perched on the end of his nose as if he were reading. He talked loudly, deafened by years in an engine room refusing to wear ear-defenders.

'Bubbles, I think these new pumps are not so good.'

'I wanted sludge pumps again, like we used in the mines,' replied Bubbles. 'But they couldn't get more of them in time.'

'They are only half the size!' Klaus went on. 'I wanted to make a bracket arrangement, so we can get them out and clean them. But Alan made me weld them into the well!'

This matched up with the little I had seen of the old pumps, when they were lifted out on to the quayside. The strain on the

28

deckhands' faces showed just how heavy they were. The new pumps were smaller, lighter and far less substantial. They also lacked a macerating blade, which would allow them to pump water thick with waste without blocking.

I couldn't help thinking that machinery that is to be depended upon is usually big and heavy. If we got into problems in stormy seas, could we really trust these pumps?

Such thoughts faded as we cast off and left Cape Town again. We motored along at nine or ten knots and the land disappeared behind us. Glen stood by the door with me for a few minutes, watching the weather outside, a cigarette in his hand. He kept his shoulders hunched, as though his small frame was perpetually cold when away from the warmth of the engine room.

For the crew of the *Sudur Havid*, the next fourteen days would be used to prepare the boat and her gear for the time ahead. Once on the fishing grounds, with thousands of pounds' worth of catch beneath us, the last thing we wanted to be doing was mending kit. The crew worked hard, watched over by the Portuguese deck-bosses, Joaquim and Carlos. Both were distinctly Mediterranean in appearance with dark eyes, dark hair and tanned skin. Joaquim was solid, ferret-faced and brusque. His English was functional, his fuse was short. Carlos was smaller and more swarthy-looking. He was quieter too, and unquestionably answered to Joaquim. With years of fishing behind them, they were more than capable of translating Boetie's orders into crew action on the decks below.

Another man worked alongside Joaquim and Carlos. Charlie was officially the same rank, bosun, but he was quietly efficient rather than explosively short-tempered. Cape Coloured with a neatly trimmed beard, friendly and professional, Charlie was well-liked and respected by the deckhands. And he was surprisingly friendly to me, given that it was his bunk that I was sleeping in.

The work may not have demanded the intense labour of fishing, but for the crew it meant long hours of uncoiling, tying, splicing, and re-coiling kilometres of rope that was to make up our long-line to catch the fish. The various components of rope, weights and buoys would eventually come together to form a line of thousands of hooks, all floating just a few metres above the seabed, and each baited with a single sardine.

In the early afternoon, I joined the crew as they worked on deck. I sat on a crate, and was introduced to Albert, Charlie's older brother, who showed me how to splice the ropes to make a loop. He was taller and more laid-back than his brother, and lacked Charlie's intense competency. Albert's eyes looked tired as he watched and patiently corrected my clumsy technique. My stomach was back to normal, and for a few warm and sunny hours it was a pleasure to chat with my new crewmates as they cut and knotted, smoked and drank a beer.

Some drank more than they worked. One of the deckhands, Alfie Clarke, was sitting on the stern deck, and greeted Boetie as he wandered down.

'Hey, Skipper! How's it?' Alfie yelled.

'Have you been drinking, Alfie?'

Alfie slowly leant further and further to one side before catching himself and sitting back upright. Bleary-eyed, he grinned, exposing the gaps where his front teeth had once been, and stroked his biker moustache.

'Do you have any more beer, Skipper?'

'You know, Alfie's not right in the head,' Boetie explained to me. 'We caught him stealing fish from the hold one day when we were in Cape Town. The refrigerant gas had leaked and he passed out. He was lucky someone found him, he could have died.'

'I wasn't stealing!' exclaimed Alfie, 'I was borrowing.'

Instead of yelling about conduct and discipline, Boetie just chuckled and walked away. Within two days of leaving Cape Town, Alfie had already finished off his booze. Whereas most of the crew had rationed their stashes, two crates of beer had disappeared down Alfie's throat. At least Boetie could now breathe a sigh of relief; Alfie would finally get on with his work.

Watching the relaxed manner in which Boetie dealt with Alfie, and the way that the crew lived and worked together on board, I knew it was going to be an interesting few months, anything but mundane.

5

THE ROARING FORTIES

Wednesday, 15 April 1998

In the wheelhouse, I stood watching the spray from the waves and the slow blink of our position on the GPS plotter. Bubbles leaned over, and pointed at our co-ordinates on the screen.

'Look, we're forty degrees south. We're officially into the Roaring Forties.'

It's an evocative name for the band of the world between 40° and 50°S. Famed for its consistent westerly winds that helped the clipper boats a hundred years ago as they circumnavigated the globe, it is equally notorious for its wild, wet weather and storms. We could expect powerful winds, driving the sea into gigantic swells.

The conditions didn't deteriorate the moment we crossed the fortieth parallel but the air was growing steadily colder, and any colour seemed to be leaching from our world. All around the boat were countless moving mounds of grey water, topped with white horses. From horizon to horizon, nothing but waves and foam flecked with the occasional charcoal bird in flight. No land offered a relief to this monotony. The sun was not strong enough, or high enough, for light to shine down into the water column. Nor was the ocean floor close enough to lend any colour or contrast.

Our course had us heading straight into the wind, which made progress slow and at times uncomfortable. There was to be no skirting areas of bad weather, or dodging swells. We just ploughed up and over every swell, or through each one, on the shortest route possible.

Within just two days, our first rough weather arrived. That evening I joined Bubbles, who was on duty in the wheelhouse. Watching the boat as she beat her way through the waves was becoming a morbid fascination for me. Into the beam of the floodlights, walls of water appeared from the darkness to engulf the bow. When the bow rose back up to the surface, the water ran across the deck and, seconds later, the spray pelted the wheelhouse windows in front of me.

Stood in the centre of the bridge, I rested one hand on the radar console. I tried to look relaxed, swaying in time with the boat, but every few minutes I was thrown off balance by a swell, and had to stagger back to my position. Bubbles, by contrast, was leaning heavily against the windows, with his arms crossed and his backside braced against the pillar of the compass binnacle. The more I watched the experienced fishermen around me, the more I noticed they were often almost motionless. While I tried to stand upright, they braced themselves against benches or leaned on the wall. My moment of comprehension was interrupted by dull thuds, coming through the metal ceiling above me.

'Go and have a look outside,' suggested Bubbles, 'they're up on the top.'

I ducked out through the starboard door, next to the life-rafts, and climbed the ladder up the side of the wheelhouse. Gripping the metal rungs, wet with spray, I peered over the lip on to the roof, the highest point of the boat.

Hannes, the beer-loving Alfie, Kenny and Little Danie were gathered at the railings around the edge, howling with excitement like children.

'Come on up, Engelsman,' yelled Hannes, 'we're playing our favourite game!'

I climbed up and held on tight to the metal guardrail. One at a time they let go and crouched, arms outstretched, in the middle of the smooth roof, trying to balance as the boat plummeted down the faces of the waves. It felt like we were in free fall, and they struggled to stay on their feet. They were surfing a fishing boat.

Later that night, I finally got invited inside one of the crew cabins. The cabins were private, so I had avoided stepping inside, but some of the deckhands wanted to show off their TV set.

Six of them shared the cabin, including Morné, Sven and Stephan, three young friends from a town called the Strand on the coast just outside Cape Town. Most of the cabins seemed to be made up of a single racial group as friends and relatives shared together.

Sven was only nineteen and the smallest in the cabin. As such, he was given the top bunk on a triple deck. He lifted his mattress to reveal all of his clothes stacked underneath. This left only a foot between the bed and the metal ceiling. He had to shuffle into his bed at night and couldn't roll over. He complained that the warm air, full of the smells of his five cabin-mates, rose to choke him and the condensation on the ceiling dripped on his face.

Stephan (pronounced 'Steven') had chosen the vacant bunk under the porthole, only to find during the first rough weather that the seals around the porthole leaked, spraying cold seawater on to his bedding. His cousin, Hannes, had lured them all on to the boat with his stories of adventure and big money.

Hannes had been on the boat for a few trips to the Southern Ocean, and as Boetie's favourite deckhand he acted as an intermediary between the crew and the bridge. One of twins and the son of a policeman, he didn't seem to have too much respect for rules and was happy to boast of his misbehaviour. Raised in the quiet farmland around Malmesbury, an hour north of Cape Town, he was just a few years older than me, blond and built like a brick shithouse. A tattoo of a panther covered his shoulder, and he had the words *Fuck Off* tattooed inside his bottom lip. Hannes had worked as a bouncer when ashore, and said that the tattoo

34

acted as a distraction for drunk trouble-makers, defusing the tension before a fight could happen. He pulled his lip out now, to show me.

'Read my lips!'

The further we moved south, the more hopeful I became that we would soon see an albatross. Each day I scanned around the boat, trying to catch my first glimpse of the spirit of the Southern Ocean. Finally, to starboard, I saw a bird in the distance skimming over the waves on long, stiff wings.

I rushed to my cabin and grabbed my heavy manual, fearful that I would lose sight of the bird. I flicked through the pages to the wildlife identification charts. The bird came low over the sea, just a metre above the shifting surface. When it was fifty metres from me, I could see the dark tops of its arced wings. Tilting a wing-tip down to the water, it turned away, and I could see its pure-white belly.

I looked at the black-and-white pictures in the file but they were almost useless; so small and fuzzy, the birds all appeared alike. My bird didn't seem to be big enough to be a wandering albatross, which I knew had a wingspan of eleven feet. It came close again and I made out its white head – which ruled out some other species – and then its pale-yellow beak. Finally I saw kohl lines slashing through its eyes. Only one species in the chart was glowering like that. It was a black-browed albatross.

Watching its aerial display, I tried to understand why it was instantly more captivating than a gull. Maybe it was its elegance, its silence, or the clear-cut definition of its colours. Maybe it was our isolation. I knew the folklore: albatrosses were the reincarnation of drowned seafarers, and to kill one brought misfortune. This bird was alert and at ease, and I was envious of it. However well I was adapting to my new home, I could never be so well-suited to this oceanic, vagabond life.

Saturday, 18 April 1998

Deep into the Roaring Forties, we now had just a thousand miles to go. Eating my breakfast in the Officers' Mess, I was struck that the boat's motion had changed as I had slept, from pitching to rolling from side to side. Sitting on the starboard bench, as I always did, I was thrown against the table one moment then pushed back in my seat the next. I caught the salt cellar as it careered towards the edge. Either we had altered course, or the swells were now coming in from a different direction. I wanted to see what was happening, so I made my way up to the wheelhouse.

The horizon was tilting thirty degrees to one side, and then thirty degrees to the other. Of all the boats I had been on before, big or small, none of them had wallowed this much. Bubbles saw my nervous glances through the side windows at the frothing water below. I must have looked alarmed, and he tried to put my mind at ease.

'It's all right, Matt, as long as she keeps rolling back!'

It felt as though the boat was tipping so far to each side that the wheelhouse windows might touch the water's surface. I knew this couldn't happen, but we seemed to go a long way over.

'Some boats move awkwardly, out of time with the swells. The *Northern Pride* used to have a really bad motion, made everyone sea-sick. This boat bobs like a duck, it's better that way when it's rough.'

Bubbles was right – she always came back up – but soon we would be into the Furious Fifties, with a reputation for even stronger winds and more frequent storms, and the risk of errant icebergs. Oceanographers describe the winds and ocean currents as circling the bottom of the globe, pushing water into larger and larger swells. With no land to block their way, the winds blow undiminished, and the waves build up and up. Sailors supposedly said: *Below forty degrees south there is no law. Below fifty degrees there is no god.*

The books I had read about the Southern Ocean had all been by people brave enough to sail there in the summer. Even Sir Robin Knox-Johnston, daft enough to set sail in 1968 around the world on his own in a thirty-two-foot wooden yacht, was sensible enough to be clear of the Southern Ocean by February. It was April, and we were about to work there through the depths of the winter.

Checking the rope crates, Sven noticed a small bundle of black feathers in among the coils of rope. The boat was the only solid object for miles, so it was little wonder that birds sometimes chose it for a resting place. He carefully picked up the seabird. Maybe it was ill, or injured? It didn't fight, or try to peck him, but just lay in his cupped hands.

'Poor thing, I'll take it somewhere warm.'

As he showed his find to Morné in his cabin, Hannes came in and caught sight of the bird.

'Jesus, you can't bring that in here!' Hannes cried, 'They're bad luck! Throw it overboard!'

'But it needs a rest . . .' Sven replied.

'It's a bad-weather bird – chuck it over the side, now!'

Sven knew there was no point in arguing against superstition, and carried the storm petrel up to the deck. He threw it into the air, and it fluttered down to land on the water. The boat sailed on, and Sven watched the little bird as it tidied its feathers, before it disappeared among the swells. It seemed unlikely that showing compassion for an animal could ever bring a curse.

10:00, Wednesday, 22 April 1998

Three weeks after the fishing season opened, we finally arrived in South Georgia. Although we had lost twenty-two days of fishing to some of the other boats, and it would be hard work to make that time up, we were excited after the passage. Standing together out on deck, the atmosphere was festive, like we'd arrived home.

After weeks of looking at a seascape of shifting grey waves, South Georgia was a feast for our eyes. The island is 120 miles long but narrow, with peaks almost 10,000 feet in height seemingly rising straight from the water. The summits were shrouded by scarves of cloud and mist as we approached, but snow and ice highlighted valleys and gullies on their flanks in the low winter light. The coves and hills were green and brown with grass and soil, and spray bounced from the rocks along the shore.

Glaciers had calved huge icebergs into the grey waters of the bay, and we watched in eagerness to see if one would actually fall before us. As though to remind us how far south we had come, sleet and snow blew across the boat, and we stuck our hands deep into our freezer suit pockets.

My home in Aberdeen was two degrees further from the equator than South Georgia, but the weather and the landscape here seemed much more extreme. With no continent to block its flow, the currents of the Southern Ocean circle west to east around Antarctica without ever being forced to visit a warmer part of the world. The Antarctic waters are freezing cold, and keep South Georgia veiled in glaciers and mountain snowfields year round.

We were required to make a brief visit to King Edward Point, a small settlement sheltered inside a cove on the north coast of the island, where the Harbour Master could inspect our vessel. I had heard that just a few dozen people lived on the island, mostly soldiers and a handful of scientists.

Chugging slowly across Cumberland Bay towards the natural inner harbour of King Edward Cove, we kept our eyes open for the 'growlers' and 'bergy-bits': car-sized icebergs almost completely submerged but still capable of damaging the hull if hit at any speed. After anchoring a few hundred metres off the land, we saw the small cluster of historic single-storey buildings and the large new accommodation block that made up the settlement of King Edward Point. Elephant seals dotted the beaches, their grey-brown boulder forms indistinct at such a distance. Across the cove from King Edward Point, the rusty derelict buildings of Grytviken reminded us of the island's previous goldrush: not fish, but whales. The flensing pans where whales were hauled ashore and carved up, and the factory sheds where the blubber was processed, were still visible through binoculars. A few old wrecks lay rusting away in the shallows, their hunting days long gone. I was glad to see the rust.

For once, Bjorgvin was awake in the daytime and stood awkwardly on the bridge. Bubbles and Boetie were visibly nervous, eager to pick up the licence and go. A failure on any point of the inspection could mean more delays and less fishing.

I had heard rumours of earlier trips, when the *Sudur Havid* had illegally poached toothfish around other islands in the Southern Ocean. These were tales of secretive unlicensed fishing, record-breaking hauls and high-seas boat chases. If word of this murky past had reached the authorities on South Georgia, the imminent scrutiny could be particularly rigorous. We may have travelled 3000 miles for a fresh start for the boat, but we needed to pass this inspection to start fishing.

Bubbles and Boetie paced restlessly as the Harbour Master was brought out to the boat by soldiers from the Royal Engineers. Their small green boat, less than twenty feet long, was dwarfed by the scenery and even by the *Sudur Havid*, but a man in a black dry suit looked relaxed as he climbed aboard and made his way up to the bridge. 'Gordon Liddle, South Georgia Harbour Master,' he announced. I couldn't quite place his Scottish accent. He unzipped his dry suit, and shrugged it down around his waist to reveal a navy jumper with epaulettes at the shoulders. 'Pleased to meet you all. Now, let's get down to business, shall we?'

Bubbles laid the ship's certificates and logs out on the navigation table, and Gordon peered at them intently, rubbing his ginger beard. He was the sole representative of the government on South Georgia, responsible for local administration as well as customs, immigration and fisheries. He started to scribble notes then passed a sheet across for Bubbles to fill in.

'This is the Icelander,' said Bubbles, gesturing at Bjorgvin, and signing his own name as Master of the vessel.

After checking the paperwork on the bridge and explaining the fishery rules, Gordon was shown around the boat by Boetie. I followed them down to the factory deck, where Gordon examined the fishing gear. First measuring the size and shape of the hooks, he then picked up one of the concrete blocks that would act as a weight. Playing it in his hands, he gauged if it was heavy enough to meet standards. When he started running the fishing line through his hands, I went back to the bridge. Bubbles was fidgeting like an expectant father.

'What's he doing, Matt? Why's he taking so long?'

Twenty minutes passed before Gordon returned to the bridge clutching his clipboard to his chest. He looked at Bubbles, who raised an eyebrow questioningly.

'Safe fishing,' Gordon said. We had the all-clear.

6

DEATH BY 15,000 HOOKS

Life on a long-liner is a game of numbers: 15,000 hooks arranged, baited, discharged and retrieved each and every day. If one man with a rod and a hook can catch one fish at a time, how many can he catch if he has a line of 15,000 hooks? The answer, by the way, is not normally 15,000 fish.

19:00, Thursday, 23 April 1998

After picking up our licence from King Edward Point, we sailed sixty miles north to the edge of the continental shelf. We would be fishing in water 800 metres deep, but just a few miles further north the seabed dropped off into the abyss. When darkness fell it was time to put our first fishing line in the water. Boats hunting for tuna, marlin or swordfish will set their long-lines to float near the surface, but we were interested in *Dissostichus eleginoides*, also known as Patagonian toothfish, which feed near the bottom.

Found from southern Chile down to the sub-Antarctic islands, including South Georgia, they are usually limited to waters where the temperature at depth does not fall below 2°C. South of these islands, beyond about 55°S, the water becomes too cold and another, similar, species, known as *Dissostichus mawsoni*, or the Antarctic toothfish, takes its place in the ecosystem.

The two species look almost identical, save for a few differences in the scales on their heads, but internally the *D. mawsoni* are adapted to carry more glycoprotein in their blood, which, as natural antifreeze, allows them to live in waters cooler than 2°C.

Although the surface water is icy around South Georgia, the temperature at depth is crucially marginally warmer, allowing the *D. eleginoides* to swim around without freezing.

Marine biologists would describe the toothfish as a mid-water predator. They hunt in the water column with their upturned mouths seeking food from the water above and around them, but not from the sea floor. Skulking at depths down to 2500 metres, they are fearsome killers. Their storm-cloud colours form a perfect camouflage, their muscular bodies equip them with speed and power, and their mouths become an inescapable trap for their prey. A profusion of thorn-sharp, recurved teeth jut out from their gums at all angles, with two rows in the top jaw and one in the bottom.

Toothfish do not have the gas-filled swim bladder that allows other fish to adjust their buoyancy to cope with changes in depth. Many deep-water species lack these and are forced either to sink to the bottom or waste energy by perpetually swimming to stay up in the water column. Instead, toothfish have changed the very composition of their bodies to become neutrally buoyant. Their skeletons and even the fringes of their scales contain more cartilage and less calcium than do shallow-water species, making them lighter. Their big, dense muscles contain large deposits of lipids, and these buoyant fats are carefully distributed through the fish's body to be most abundant near the centres of gravity and buoyancy. At their largest, the streamlined and powerfully finned toothfish can reach well over a hundred kilos in weight and two metres in length. They are an abyssal cruise missile with a toothy grin.

Their nostrils and taste buds strain to pick up the drifting flavours of mucus that tell them a meal is nearby. The gently bowed lateral lines that resemble knife scars along their sides, and that give them the name *Dissostichus* (separating lines), monitor the still water for pressure waves from the panic of disturbed prey.

Sensory canals on their heads perform a similar purpose, detecting water vibration and temperature changes. Using their large eyes to search for pinpricks of light, the toothfish patrols the gullies and crests, waiting for those giveaway flicker reflections of biolumin-escence from their prey's scales. The juvenile toothfish and defenceless grenadiers, squid and crabs make for a nutritious if sparse diet. At the low temperatures in which they live, with a metabolism to rival that of a corpse, food would not need to come often, but with time they grow large. It takes a toothfish nine or ten years to reach maturity, when it can reproduce, at which point it is about three feet long and its only predators are elephant seals and sperm whales. The seventy-kilo fish we were hoping to catch may well have been alive for thirty, forty or even fifty years.

Slow-growing and slow-living, toothfish spend their whole lives in the pure, chilled waters of the Southern Ocean. This, combined with their formidable muscles developed for hunting, makes them delicious to eat and one of the ultimate examples of organic pro-duce. You won't find toothfish for sale in any fishmonger's or restaurant. Who would want to buy 'toothfish' for dinner? 'Here we are, darling, toothfish and chips.'

What about 'Chilean sea bass'? That sounds much better. Once it is rebranded you can order, for twice the price of rump steak and only at the most exclusive dining tables around the world, a piece of an ugly, oversized, buck-toothed fish that never saw the light of day.

Boetie explained that we were fishing a bottom-set 'Spanish' long-line, which uses a weighted rope mainline to take the strain and a set of parallel fishing lines to hold the hooks, each of which dangles on its own little branch line or 'snood'. The lines float just above the seabed, and create a wall of baited hooks from which the scent can drift down-current. Boetie believed that this was the most effective way of long-lining and meant that we could make incremental changes to each component of the line. However, it was also one of the most labour-intensive methods. I had seen autoliners (with automated retrieval, baiting and discharge systems) in Scotland and they seemed to take a lot of repetitive work out of the process. Labour on our boat was cheap though and hand baiting meant that he knew each and every hook was properly prepared.

If the baited hooks were deployed during the day, albatrosses and other birds could be lured to their deaths as they tried to gorge on the 15,000 baited sardines they see, and the 15,000 hooks they don't. Natural selection has attuned their senses to seek out small silvery prey in the vast ocean. Long-liners, therefore, present a parade of irresistible silvery flashes every time they set their lines. On the *Sudur Havid*, the line would be sent plummeting to the seabed after nightfall, in order to catch the fish during the night and early hours of the morning. It would be retrieved over the course of the following day, and processed as it came aboard.

Nearing the first of our chosen positions, the crew prepared to set the line. On the bridge, Boetie stared ahead into the darkness, watching the waves and the froth hurl themselves at the toughened glass in front of him. I needed to be right at the stern, observing the seabirds, so I wrapped myself in as many layers as possible under my deck-suit, and pulled my woolly hat down over my ears. The air was cold tonight. In the alley between the crates of rope eight of the crew were waiting, kitted up in oilskins, their faces hidden by scarves and balaclavas. They were eager to start. Trevor stood by the door, tucking his gloves in under his oilskin sleeves. He was in his forties but seemed older than most of the other crew on board. Cape Coloured, with a bushy beard, he was quick to joke and never complained. His smile now reassured me. 'Are you ready, Matt?'

I realized that shooting the line could be a dangerous operation for me. I needed a good view but there would be ropes under tension and hooks zipping through the air, as well as the risk of falling overboard. I didn't have a deck lifejacket, but neither, I saw, looking around, did anyone else. The boat was operating with a minimum number of lights, and this meant that the stern deck was disconcertingly dark. I had found myself a small corner, just to one side of the stern, which had a wooden shelf that I could stand on. Shuffling past Sven and Trevor, I used Hannes' shoulder as I climbed up. Joaquim barked some simple instructions. 'Matt, you stand still up there. Don't move, and watch out for ropes and hooks.'

The wind was blowing strongly and the boat was pitching and rolling on the swells. At least with my feet braced against the guardrail and my back against the crates, I was stable and sheltered from the gusts and the spray.

Joaquim threw the buoy of the bird streamer line overboard, and the fifty metres of rope paid out. The boat towed the buoy along, and it danced around on the end of the rope, shaking strips of ribbon and tape that decorated it. This simple arrangement was designed to scare away the seabirds, to stop them from hovering over the back of the boat.

Without ceremony, Joaquim next wrestled our first marker buoys of the season over the side. Trevor and Sven fed out the anchor rope, throwing bundles still half coiled into the water. In total, this was a mile of rope, twice the depth of the water we were in. Hannes and Morné stood waiting, struggling to balance the two 45kg steel-plate anchors on the rail of the boat, while the anchor chains rested at their feet. At Joaquim's signal, they let go and the anchors tumbled overboard with a metallic clang and rattle of the chain. Starting their descent to the seabed, the anchors dragged the 20mm mainline rope with them. The boat steamed away at six knots and the crew tied on the fishing lines as the mainline fed out from the stern.

At intervals, thinner ropes called 'droppers' had been attached to the mainline. Joaquim passed the end of the first dropper down to Carlos, who was sheltered in the factory below. Carlos tied it with a fisherman's knot to the end of a rope hanging from a basket, and a concrete weight. These knots were tied quickly, cold fingers fumbling the rope, before the mainline was dragged over the stern by the anchor and the progress of the vessel.

The 150 individual fishing lines, each coiled in its own giant plastic tub, were made of much thinner rope than the mainline. They were readied by the pot-makers on the boat, including Stephan, who neatly coiled the rope around the perimeter of its tub and arranged each of the hundred hooks around the lip. Each hook's metre-long monofilament snood was coiled in the centre. Care and precision ensured that the line came out without tangling.

Just before the boat began shooting the line, the hooks had been baited with a sardine. These dangled around the rim of the tub like a bejewelled necklace, with each hook piercing the eyes of the bait. They were quite beautiful in their careful arrangement, until the moment they were attached to the line and became a blur of uncoiling rope and flying fish. The tub containing the fishing line was held at a 60° angle by Charlie at the stern hatch of the factory deck, which allowed each of the baited hooks to disappear into the night: thousands of single sardines flying as nature never intended before plunging into the sea, towed to the depths by the anchor and numerous weights. Once each tub had paid out, Carlos tied another knot to join the fishing line back to the mainline. One by one, we attached all of the 150 fishing lines in this way.

My only duty during this whole two-hour process was to watch, and to light an occasional cigarette for a crewman whose hands were busy. One fag at a time was best; lighting four at once made me dizzy. I reached for the packet tucked in the back of Morné's woolly hat, and then put the lit cigarette in his mouth. Morné was the same age and build as me, and it was his first deep-sea trip as well. He growled out a deep 'Dankie' (thanks), and inhaled deeply.

For the deckhands, with watches hidden under layers of clothing, the passing of time was marked not in hours but in cigarettes.

I had expected the process to be noisy, but the crew on deck worked almost silently with just a few requests or yells of command from Joaquim. I could see loops of rope forming, tightening and disappearing as they were pulled overboard. Occasional stray hooks flailed upwards or became tangled in the lines.

Hannes leant over the rusty guardrail to hand the end of a rope to the deck below when a hook snagged his jacket arm. Within seconds, the fishing line began to tighten. He wouldn't stand a chance if he was pulled overboard, whether he could swim or not. The water was just above zero, and the shock of the cold water would probably kill him before he could be freed. Within ten metres of the boat he would disappear into the ink of the night, no floodlights to illuminate his flailing arms as the anchor and weights towed him under, like a sardine bait in cheap oilskins. Even the weakest component, the nylon monofilament snood holding the hook, was strong enough to hold a struggling hundred-kilo toothfish underwater, which was plenty strong enough to pull a man overboard and down.

Near my feet, a knife stood with its tip embedded in the wood of the bench. I had guessed that it was there for emergencies. It would take minutes to alert the bridge and to stop and turn the boat around as it steamed at six knots. Even if Hannes managed to free himself of the line in the water, I reasoned that he would flounder and drown before he could be found in the darkness.

'Wo! Wo! Wo!' Hannes cried out.

His voice rang out over the thrum of the engine and the wind. The line went tight. Joaquim grabbed the knife and leant over the guardrail. Moments before Hannes was dragged overboard, the thin nylon sprang apart under the blade.

The cries of relief were muffled by thick scarves, and the line carried on overboard as normal.

'*Caralho!*' came Joaquim's supportive Portuguese reply – '*Cock!*'

Crisis averted, I forced myself further back into my little corner. Joaquim was right. I was safest when I was tucked back away from the lines. I was required to observe for an hour every time the line was set, but there were too many dangers and distractions for comfort. Once all of the 15,000 hooks had been deployed, another anchor would be attached to the mainline and dropped over the side, with a rope and buoys, and the ship could sail away to leave the line on the seabed.

Making my way back inside to get warm, I saw Bubbles frowning at the waves through the bridge windows that faced astern, as if trying to prevent an accident by sheer willpower. It seemed that Boetie worried more about the fishing, while Bubbles was more concerned about the crew.

That night, Bjorgvin kept watch on the bridge while we slept, and the oily scent from the sardines drifted in the current across the seabed hundreds of metres below.

07:00, Friday, 24 April 1998

Hauling the line needed to start at first light; it would take eight to ten hours to complete and we had to be ready to shoot away again in the evening.

Once the boat drew alongside the buoys, Sven threw a grappling hook overboard to snag the line between the markers, and pulled them on deck. He passed the anchor line to Walu Walu, who flicked it around the capstan of the massive winch. From half a mile below the surface, the anchors were slowly retrieved. They surfaced about an hour later and were carried back along the boat between Hannes and Trevor, who struggled to keep their footing on the moving deck. With the anchors stowed, the line was gradually reeled in from the starboard side of the *Sudur Havid* and 'unzipped', a process in which each individual fishing line was untied from the mainline.

The winch on the main deck hauled in the mainline, while a line hauler set into the factory deck below pulled in the thinner fishing lines with their hooks. Within the line hauler, a rotating drum held pistons which squeezed the line and held it while the drum turned, pulling it without tangling the hooks. The hooks passed through rollers that yanked them from the mouths of any fish caught, which slumped down a chute into the factory.

Joaquim and Carlos usually operated the line hauler to control its speed and to sort out any tangles that inevitably occurred in kilometres of line. The line hauler pit was entered by a heavy waterproof door from the factory, and sealed by handles called 'dogs'. Most waterproof doors on a boat are fitted to open outwards, so that a wave striking them will push them against their frame to form an even more effective seal against the pressure of the water. But this one opened inwards, making it weaker. To add to its vulnerability, the door was tied open when we were fishing.

I watched from the rail as the fish came up out of the water. Boetie explained that if you let the winch haul a large toothfish out of the water using only the hook that caught it, there is a risk you will lose it. The weight of the big fish, or their struggles, could rip the hooks from their mouths. What you need is a man with a gaff – preferably someone with good hand–eye co-ordination and enough upper-body strength. Hannes fitted the bill, and he knew it.

Hannes leant over the side of the boat, wielding the three-metre-long bamboo gaff like a spear. When each fish broke the surface, he jabbed the six-inch-long hook on the end of the pole down into the water and then up into the fish's gill slits, lifting it on to the aluminium chute that led into the factory. With nonchalance, he hooked the fish accurately to avoid damaging the valuable flesh, and worked with the winches to flick the fish aboard.

The water around the boat was now full of hopeful spectators, all at risk of being snagged on a hook. Even in these confused swells, the northern giant petrels bobbed expectantly, waiting for a dropped fish or a scrap of bait to fall from the line.

Airborne, the giant petrels were almost as elegant as an albatross. Silent and stiff-winged, they measured roughly two metres across. Once on the water, however, their mystique disappeared as they scavenged for scraps. With their speckled brown and ash plumage, and incessant jeering and croaking, they resembled medieval hags in sackcloth barging through a teeming market place.

In their midst were black-browed albatrosses and smaller Cape petrels. Rare wandering albatrosses flew in on broadsword wings, to land clumsily nearby. Their massive white bodies stood out among the crowd, and their beaks cleared a space around them. Occasional macaroni penguins popped up. It was difficult not to smile as I watched them bickering with the other birds, looking simultaneously comical but furious due to the unruly crests of yellow feathers over their eyes. I wondered how the birds had found us so soon after we started fishing.

When a toothfish bigger than me broke the surface, Hannes called out, 'Trevor, Sven, come quickly, big fish!'

Gravity distorted the massive fish's torpedo shape, its gut sagging to form an obese bulge and its mouth pulled open to reveal a staggering array of teeth. It twitched on the line, barely alive, its scales dull grey-brown in the harsh daylight.

A fish worth hundreds of pounds, it could easily be ripped off the hook by its own weight and lost back into the sea. Joaquim grabbed his video camera as Carlos slowed the line-hauler and Trevor and Sven ran to Hannes' side. They grabbed gaffs from the deck and leant out over the rail. All three of them working together now, they hauled the impressive monster over the edge of the boat and on to the chute. Its head promptly wedged in the hatch, the tail flapped overboard and Carlos pushed it through into the factory below me.

From his chair up on the bridge, Boetie watched the hauling process and tried to adjust the position of the *Sudur Havid*, so that the line was almost vertical. If the line came too far underneath the boat it might rub against the hull, risking the loss of fish and wasting hooks to decorate the underside of the boat. If it fell too far behind the *Sudur Havid* there was the risk of tangling the mainline in the propeller, the results of which could be catastrophic, potentially disabling the boat. But if the line was too far ahead of the boat or too far out to the side, too much tension could be placed on the ropes and they might snap. Boetie's eyes barely left the line or the deck as we talked in the wheelhouse. Serious about his fishing, the jokes and light-heartedness ended abruptly as soon as he noticed someone slacking at the front of the boat. Fuse lit, his voice exploded over the loudspeaker.

'Hannes, what the fuck are you doing? Gaff all the fish, all of them, that's money you've just dropped!'

From the line hauler pit, each fishing line, with its hundred hooks, passed through the hatches into the factory, where Grant coiled it roughly into a basket. At twenty-two, Grant was one of the younger deckhands. He was Cape Coloured, short and slight with a thin pencil moustache, a jester always louder than his colleagues. He came on the boat to spend more time with his father, Brian, who was always away fishing when Grant was growing up. Although Brian worried that his son was not built for the ocean life, Grant bounced around the factory with such energy and noise that he was hard to miss.

After Grant looped the line loosely into a basket it was ready for Stephan and the other pot-makers to untangle, arrange and re-coil in preparation for shooting again in the evening. The fine manipulation of the thin monofilament snoods and hooks required the pot-makers to work without gloves, even though the air in the factory was freezing. Doing this important and skilled job, the Namibian pot-makers were some of the worst-paid people on the boat. Some of the crew had blown their advances in the bars and brothels of Cape Town, so it would take them much of the trip before they would earn any money.

Although Bubbles and Boetie seemed to be respected and popular with the crew, the distinction between the bridge and the decks was staggering. Two or three metres of physical distance, but a gulf in comfort and reward. Golf jackets, jogging bottoms, hundred-thousand-dollar incomes and penthouse apartments for those on the bridge; drenched oilskins, damp freezer suits and twenty dollars a week on the decks below.

16:00, Friday, 24 April 1998

For the next hour I was in the factory collecting samples and measuring the fish as they came aboard. After the clear air and panorama of the main deck, the factory was noisy and claustrophobic. The rumble and whine of the engine and the winches, and the constant roar of the waves and the wind outside, joined with the clatter and laughter of twenty working men. The air was so cold in the unheated factory that any smells were subdued, and the fresh seawater washed away any stale odours of men, bait or catch. The way in which the crew of the *Sudur Havid* dealt with the fish was simply stunning. Processing went on all day as the line was hauled and, within an hour of being lifted still breathing from the water, the fish were headed, gutted, washed and into the freezer. Three months later, almost as fresh as the day they were caught, they could be offloaded to port or another boat, and then off to market.

Each fish that came down the chute from the line hauler was usually alive, and was seized by Mark with a thumb in one eye and a finger in the other. He rolled the fish on to his bench and on to its belly, and made a quick incision down through the neck from just behind the head, curving backwards towards the tail. Mark called this a J cut, due to the curve towards the tail, which allowed the gut of the fish to be removed with minimum waste.

The head was thrown to one side and the tail was cut off and then discarded. Any waste was kept in plastic fish boxes until the end of the day, when it could be thrown overboard without attracting the attention of the seabirds. With no proper storage, much of it ended up on the factory floor.

The body of the fish was passed on to Alfie, one of the gutters. His job was to quickly scoop out the insides and clean the cavity, before passing it to Big Danie, who was a washer. Big Danie cleansed the inside of the fish with a brush and cold fresh seawater, and then placed it into a white plastic fish bin. Finally, Morné took each fish and wrapped a noose of string around the tail-end before hanging it on one of the three rows of hooks on the scaffolding racks of the blast freezer, where the cold air could circulate freely around them. Monster fish, which were too big for the racks, would be placed on the floor.

The crew were not interested in processing the other species of fish that had been caught, including a small number of rays, grenadiers ('rat-tails'), blue antimora, stone crabs and other deep-water oddities, none of which had any real value in the marketplace. Most of them went back over the side, dead, but the crabs were passed to Grunter. We would eat them later.

If Mark and Alfie had time, the heads of the fish would later be taken and trimmed to remove the 'collar' of the fish. This was the throat and 'shoulders', and formed the muscular attachment to the pectoral fins. The cheeks of the fish could be cut out with the twist of a knife. These small packs of muscle are renowned for their flavour and fine texture, and are particularly valuable. On a toothfish, they are also particularly large in order to operate its huge jaws. All of this extra meat was to be frozen and kept as a bargaining chip, undeclared to the company offices in Cape Town.

Bubbles had a plan that it would be used to ensure an extra bonus for the crew.

By five o'clock in the evening, we had finished hauling the line. While Mark cut the cheeks from the gory pile of toothfish heads, I cleaned up the small bone samples I had collected. I wiped each of the tiny otoliths, the ear bones of the toothfish, with a tissue and placed them in envelopes. I had been dreading the start of fishing, apprehensive that I wouldn't be able to keep up with the pace of the crew, or would disrupt their work and routine. Now these feelings were beginning to dissipate. I had stayed out of harm's way, at least so far.

7

TOO FAR FROM HOME

Monday, 27 April 1998

I was told I would be at sea for three months but it was now becoming clear that I was expected to stay for the whole fishing season, which meant I could be on the *Sudur Havid* until mid-September. I tried to draw on the positives – I was having an adventure, after all – but I was missing home and the freedom of dry land.

With no heating in the mess, and the air temperatures outside routinely as low as – 7°C, I grew used to the sight of my breath at mealtimes. At each meal my food slid on the plate and, despite a non-slip mat, the plate slid on the table. To adapt, I ate with one hand, keeping the plate still and my drink upright with the other. I locked my legs under the bench for stability.

In my bunk at night, if I relaxed too much I rolled with the swells, which made my bunk squeak and woke me up. If I braced against the swell, or if I thought about the movement, I couldn't sleep either. The best solution was normally to lie on my back, but in rough weather the boat would roll so much that I almost fell out of my bunk. The noise and the rocking only stopped on a few precious nights, when the ocean was calm enough for Klaus to turn off the engines to save fuel. Then, we would drift off to sleep on the currents, the din of the engines replaced by silence.

There were some moments of comedy, of course, such as Simon the Steward getting his daily electric shock. There's nothing to lighten your mood like watching a crewmate getting zapped by a faulty electrical device. In an effort to improve security, an unknown perpetrator – probably Melvin – had decided to put a padlock on the fridge and a screw through something important to produce an electrically live fitting. Simon came up regularly from the kitchen to collect odd supplies from the fridge in the Officers' Mess, but his work as Steward/kitchen assistant seemed to leave him with permanently damp hands from washing dishes downstairs. Perhaps he felt out of place with all of the whiteys upstairs, but Simon was always nervous, and looked like a wildebeest calf in the company of a pride of lions. His nervousness meant that he usually sidled into the room, reached slowly for the door of the fridge with his cold clammy hands . . . before 'ZAP!'

I couldn't really complain about a few more months away to those around me. Brian had been at sea since he was twelve years old, and some of the crew had lived like this for over thirty years. They had spent more time on these tiny boats than with their families. Bubbles and Boetie were both married with children. For them, the money was obviously good, and meant that they could afford beautiful homes and expensive lifestyles for their loved ones, but was it worth missing their kids growing up? I wondered about the deckhands, who earned less and saved less. What would happen to their families if fishing lived up to its dangerous reputation? Who would provide for them?

In a quiet moment one evening Bubbles added that, for some of the crew, life at sea could be the only way to make a marriage work. The long periods apart could keep an incompatible relationship alive, or at least prolong it by a few more years. Golden homecomings and short spells ashore could be used to start families and build memories to sustain a husband through his time at sea, nine months out of twelve.

For much of our own trip we had been out of contact with our loved ones. The *Sudur Havid* had a basic Inmarsat satellite connection that allowed emails and faxes to be sent, but phone calls were not possible. Messages were typed slowly on a clunky communications computer on the bridge, its grey screen blinking as Bubbles read over our shoulders. Even then, only the young and computer-literate among us, who felt comfortable asking, were allowed to send a fax or email home. Two grey buttons marked 'DISTRESS' on the beige terminal caught my attention every time I typed. Bubbles explained that, if pressed and held simultaneously, they would trigger a signal to the maritime rescue authorities. It was reassuring to know we had such technology on board.

Bubbles offered me a ship-to-shore call to Corinne, via the land station at Portishead just a few miles from my family home near Bristol, but low atmospheric pressure had weakened the signal. I held off, saving the call for a special occasion, and instead typed out a fax of our change of plan to Corinne's work office. Her reply would be relayed to the boat via the office in Cape Town.

27 APR 1998 18:01

as far as a date for homecoming, it's really too early to say . . . if the fishing stays this way, they've said they may cut the trip short. but (and brace yourself for this) if the fishing is good they can stay until the licence ends on aug 31. what they didn't tell me is that i'm obliged to stay on board until they finish. either way, i don't get a choice – it's up to the skippers to decide when we get back to cape town, but I thought i'd warn you. missing you loads, love matt

Tuesday, 28 April 1998

It was my twenty-fourth birthday and, although we were busy fishing, there was still the opportunity to mark the occasion with special food and alcohol. At lunchtime, Grunter cooked me a hand-sized chunk of toothfish as a surprise. I had never eaten it before and stared at the pure-white flesh, pulling the flakes apart with my fork. The mild, delicate flavour was pleasant but the texture was fatty and felt soft against my tongue; Bubbles mentioned that it was better when smoked. I couldn't help thinking that this fish wasn't worth risking our lives for so far from home.

A two-metre-long porbeagle shark was dead when she came on board that afternoon, her tail tangled in the mainline. She was carrying four pups in her abdomen, each a perfect little shark, each with a yolk sac still attached. I convinced Hannes not to eat the babies. Although they were dead, it seemed inhumane and I threw them over the side. The mother, however, was to be turned into shark biltong and strips of her flesh were cut away to be marinated in Worcester sauce and dried in the funnel. The flesh was translucent when cured, and tasted vaguely like diesel.

Before the carcass was dumped back into the sea, I pulled open her mouth and looked inside: her jaws were lined with razor-sharp teeth. While the crew finished processing and cleaning, I cut the jaws out and sat in the factory carefully plucking them clean. The soft flesh between the growing inner teeth was particularly fiddly. With the jaws cleaned, I hung them up to dry. They would make a gruesome souvenir.

In the evening, after the line had been set for the night, it was time for my first hard lesson on the boat. Bubbles and Boetie kept a good supply of red wine, brandy and whisky in a closely guarded cupboard next to the stairs of the bridge. Given an excuse to break loose for a few hours, Boetie suggested a game of Rummikub and some drinks. Big and Little Danie, Hannes, Mark and several others joined us downstairs in the crew's mess. So close to the kitchen, the smell of fried food and coffee loitered long after the last meal. We laid out the board game on one of the well-worn melamine tables and sat on the hard benches on either side while Boetie explained the rules to me.

At the table, I found myself in a dangerous position with Boetie to one side and Hannes to the other. Both were big drinkers and generous with their measures, and I knew it would be difficult to keep up.

'You know, Matt, we South Africans don't get to drink much of this KWV brand, most of it is for export. It's nice, eh?' said Boetie, wielding the bottle of pinotage.

Once the first drinks were poured and the game had started, it was easy to forget that we were on a little boat miles from land. By the time I had learnt the rules, several bottles of wine had been finished, and we moved on to brandy and coke. As Boetie got drunker, the drinks were getting stronger. For all my pleading, there were to be no half-measures.

'Matt, if you want to play with the boys, go out in the yard.'

'It's all right, it's not like we'll be working hard tomorrow. We've got it easy right now,' said Hannes. 'When I was poaching off Kerguelen, we were catching twenty tonnes a day!'

I balked. Twenty tonnes a day made the tonne or two we were catching look like child's play.

'The catches were huge!' said Grant 'We had to clear them before the next line was hauled, and I was so tired I fell asleep standing up!'

'When the *Praia* was caught close to us, we had to run.' Hannes was getting into his stride. 'We thought the French gunboat was chasing us, so we had the lights out, scrubbing the decks and chucking the hooks and gear over the side.'

'We were pushing the boat so hard,' Bubbles chipped in from the doorway, 'the engineers were worried that the engine would blow up. They were running up and down the stairs checking the temperatures. I've never seen a Chief move so fast!'

Big Danie staggered back in with a bottle of J&B – the move from brandy to whisky sealed our livers' fates.

'Ek dink die Engelsman raak dronk!' he said.

'Speak English, man,' Boetie yelled. 'Matt can't understand!'

Big Danie was right. The Englishman was drunk, very drunk. The narrow corridors of the boat helped me on the short climb back to my cabin.

I woke the next morning to find that I had thrown up into my favourite running shoes, and had covered the floor next to my bunk. A single footprint in the centre of the puddle marked my cabin-mate's exit at the start of his 07:00 shift. Rehydrating proved even more unpleasant. The water on board tasted foul and was made from seawater using the heat of the engines. I couldn't drink a glass on its own and made cup after cup of tea instead. With the unrelenting bob of the boat, I realized I could take days to recover, but the hangover was worth it. I was supposed to be an objective Observer; now I was feeling more like one of the crew.

By early May, and after two weeks of fishing, the mood on the boat was restless. Catches just weren't up to expectations and the feeling was that we should try new grounds. In the factory, Mark's workstation for cutting off heads was positioned close to the hatch where I measured and sampled the fish. His dark beard and intense stare made him look overly solemn and intimidating, but he had lots to talk about.

'I'm thinking you and I are brewing up some bad karma.'

'In what way?' I asked.

'It's always you or me who kill the fish; it can't be good for the soul. I didn't have to kill things when I was a welder.'

With a wife and young son back in Cape Town, he was keen to earn some money and return home as soon as possible. But with catches as poor as they were, the pay cheque would be far lower than expected.

'I won't be doing this job again in a hurry,' he muttered, 'Not for no money. We need to catch more than a tonne a day!'

Boetie mentioned quitting South Georgia altogether, but with so much invested in the licence he chose instead to search for richer pastures nearby. Fishermen in the UK often work a familiar patch. Generations of a family may have fished the same waters, and their knowledge of the fishes' lives and the underwater topography grows with each season. When combined with shallower seas and improving sonar technology, this means they can visualize the sea-mounts, canyons, rocks, wrecks and sandbanks that make up their hunting grounds. We, on the other hand, were exploring an enormous area using only a tired old echo-sounder and diaries provided by Captain Andreas of the *Northern Pride*, recorded from just a season's fishing a decade before.

Bubbles and Boetie listened with great interest to any radio conversations between the Skippers on the fishery, or between Observers, and even to the daily and weekly catch reports required by Gordon, Harbour Master on South Georgia. Wily captains chose to transmit their catch statistics and fishing positions in other more confidential forms, by fax or email, but older boats and those with equipment problems sometimes had to call in their catches over the HF radio. Such nuggets of news were readily received by the other Skippers. When our turn to report came up, Bubbles burst into song, 'Oh, Flower of Scotland', for the pleasure of the Scottish Harbour Master. Maybe it was Bubbles' Irish roots, but he could do a reasonable Scottish accent, and had a surprisingly good baritone.

Boats reporting better catches than ours were believed to be near Shag Rocks, a hundred miles north-west of South Georgia. When Bubbles checked Andreas' logs, the region had proved plentiful years before, and could hold just the right balance of food and gullies so beloved of the toothfish. If we dropped the line through an area rich with fish, we would soon make up for the day lost in the journey.

14:00, Thursday, 7 May 1998

Bubbles called me up to the bridge – something large was showing up on the radar. Due to our low viewpoint disappearing into the troughs of the swells, it was difficult to see any distance ahead. Surely it couldn't be Shag Rocks; we still had miles to go.

Drawing nearer, the object dominated the radar screen. We were familiar with the fading marks left by large swells, or the small blip of a distant fishing boat, but this was many hundreds of metres across and unmoving. Through the gloom, a white cliff caught the light. For an object so pure, it projected a surprising malevolence. We had seen just a few icebergs on our trip, and this giant was the largest by far. In a world of shifting horizontal planes, the towering white precipice reflected the low sunlight to catch the eye, proud against the grey sea.

Those on the bridge were expected to be vigilant for icebergs, even at night. Not all of them would show up on radar. No one wanted to test the steel of the *Sudur Havid*'s hull in a collision. Bubbles watched as though it might suddenly pounce on us, only relaxing once the iceberg faded behind us some hours later.

If any of us were expecting something to see when we arrived at Shag Rocks, we were to be disappointed. I had imagined fishing next to a mount rising from the sea. Some of the cliffs rise seventy metres from the water, but we were fishing forty miles south-east, where the seabed dropped away into the abyssal depths.

The following morning, as the line came aboard, a large fin broke the surface of the water by the side of the boat. A pressure wave then moved forward along the hull, in the opposite direction to the swells. Watching the bulge in the sea's surface, a shape materialized. Where there had been water before there was now a killer whale, just a few feet below me, charging on its side. I beamed.

The orca were not popular with the crew and were known to

steal fish from the line, but I had been waiting to see them all trip; I tried to restrain my excitement. The fishing line twanged and Hannes swore as the whale plucked a toothfish from the hook just before it broke the surface. A dangling pair of fishy lips was all that remained on the hook, taunting the fishermen. The whale was not black and white, but brown and cream, like a sixties retro version. The tint is due to a film of diatoms (planktonic algae) that builds up on the whales' skin in the Antarctic waters. No less intimidating than their northern cousins, they usually arrive in pods of seven to ten animals. There are several types of killer whales recognized in the Southern Ocean. Some are bigger, and are thought to specialize in attacking minke whales. Others patrol the edge of the ice pack hunting seals. The killer whale now lurking around our boat was of the type thought to eat mostly fish – two thirds of its diet – with seals making up most of the remainder. Toothfish would normally be out of their reach in the depths, but now they were like sushi on a fourteen-kilometre conveyor belt.

More orca appeared, as the rest of the pod joined in. We were losing more to the whales than we were hauling aboard. I looked up to see a whale, fifty metres off to starboard, throwing a large fish into the air.

'Bastards, they steal our fish!' Joaquim protested.

There was nothing the fishermen could do but move. Joaquim attached a buoy to the mainline before cutting the rope, and we sailed away in the faint hope of losing the whales' attention. An hour later, we began hauling from the other end of the line. It didn't work. The killer whales reappeared as the anchor came on deck; they could move far more quickly than us. The water-borne noises of the boat had given away our position instantly. In the past, the crew had used thunder flashes – small explosive charges like fireworks that create an underwater shock – to scare away whales. But that had stopped on the *Sudur Havid* a few years earlier due to a small accident. Grunter, the cook, had been in charge of lighting the fuses and throwing the fireworks overboard. On the fishing grounds off Namibia, he had knocked the blowtorch over, igniting the whole pile of thunder flashes. Now the crew had no means to scare them, but just had to hope they would get bored or full, and move away.

It was easy to admire the orca. While we rolled for days on end on a slow metal hulk, wrapped from head to toe in stuffy insulation, they charged through the water, stole fish from our line with casual accuracy, and then went off to play with their spoils within sight of the boat.

13:00, Saturday, 9 May 1998

Our catches rose from under one and a half tonnes a day to three tonnes at Shag Rocks. This was the weight of the final product, once headed and gutted. Three-tonne days therefore meant lifting almost five tonnes of fish aboard, which was enough to keep the gaffers and gutters busy. It wasn't the goldmine that some of the crew had seen around Kerguelen, but it was enough to start having a noticeable effect on the empty void of the hold, and even Mark was smiling.

The fish were coming aboard slowly in the early afternoon, and Hannes took the chance to show Little Danie how to gaff. Happily ensconced as a greaser, Danie was no longer a threat to the position of alpha hunter, so Hannes passed him the bamboo pole.

Danie struggled to get the timing and action right, and Joaquim swore abuse at him from the line hauler: he missed fish after fish. Boetie yelled over the loudspeaker:

'Send the cripple back to the engine room!'

Hannes stepped forward to help but Danie jerked the gaff upwards, accidentally striking Hannes in the eye. He reeled away, and his hand shot up to his face. Blood trickled down his cheek.

'Jesus, Danie, what the hell have you done?'

Climbing slowly up the bridge, clutching his bloodied face, Hannes was convinced he was blind. Boetie tried to calm his favourite deckhand, gently pulling away his shaking fingers. The gaff had ripped open a ragged one-centimetre-long tear in Hannes' eyelid. Luckily, the pole had just missed the eyeball but it was still a sickening wound that could easily get infected – we were 700 miles from the nearest medical centre.

There was no way Boetie was going to stop fishing and take the boat all the way to the Falkland Islands just for Hannes' eyelid. Bubbles made an unlikely nurse, but first aid was his responsibility. In the Officers' Mess, Hannes sat while Bubbles cleaned the wound, and dressed it with a bulky pad and metres of tape. With no better option, he decided to give Hannes a day off.

Hannes was soon working back on deck with an eyepatch but his gaffing went astray. After a few days of watching fish dropping back into the sea and then swimming away, he tore off the patch in frustration. The red jagged rip in his eyelid would have to heal exposed to the fresh sea air.

One week later I was up in the wheelhouse, chatting with Bubbles. I leant against the desk and typed out a fax to Corinne on the satellite communications computer. I tried to keep it upbeat, knowing that she worried about me, but it was difficult to be funny when I was homesick, and when there was no exclamation mark on the keyboard. Bubbles pulled out his pack of Texan Plain cigarettes. He smoked filter cigarettes for his wife, who was worried about his lungs, but flicked off the filter before lighting them. Hannes limped on to the bridge, holding his stomach.

'Skipper, I'm not feeling too good. I think I've got a kidney infection.'

Hannes waved a drinking glass in front of Bubbles, full of what looked like urine flecked with blood. Bubbles looked panicked; he didn't know what to do. He faxed the office, and asked for some advice. The boat carried virtually no medicines, other than painkillers. In the meantime, the best he could offer was a couple of days off and a very limited supply of sympathy. Hannes returned to his bunk, and only surfaced to shuffle around looking ill. Earlier in the trip Hannes had spoken of his father's early death, and of his fear that he and his twin had inherited the same weak heart. For all his strength and bravado, Hannes was troubled by the idea that he would die young. I was concerned something was gravely wrong, and found myself wanting to yell at Bubbles. If Hannes was pissing blood then he needed professional medical help.

But Hannes recovered, very suddenly, and went back to work. The truth came out, days later. While looking for eye cream in the medical kit, Hannes had discovered some hypodermic syringes. He withdrew some blood from his arm and laced his urine sample. Feigning life-threatening illness was probably the only way to get out of work.

Boetie laughed it off, and threatened to dock his wages, but there was something unsettling about the whole incident. Bubbles' response to the crisis had worried me. It would have taken days for us to reach a hospital, and we were so remote that even a helicopter medical evacuation was out of the question. Hannes had highlighted just how isolated we were, how far from assistance of any form. What if something went dangerously wrong, so far from help?

8

LAST SIGHT

I came out on deck to find a sperm whale just off the bow, rolling sleepily in the water like a giant pebble, as though it had been alongside the boat for company through the night. Joaquim and Trevor crossed their fingers, hoping that the whale would disappear before the fish started coming aboard. The whale stirred and dived for the depths; I watched as its tail rose into the classic silhouette.

After nearly two months away at sea our fuel was running low but the hold was only half-full – fifty-five tonnes, out of a possible hundred. In fishing terms we were behind, and a few weeks off our scheduled halfway landing. Rather than returning to Cape Town, the company were toying with the idea of a stop in Montevideo, Uruguay, or Punta Arenas, Chile. Alan Newman, back in Cape Town, seemed to spend days weighing up the time and cost of reaching the port, refuelling, replenishing the food stores, and of any maintenance required, versus the price that could be achieved for the toothfish. Bubbles typed out replies to Alan's daily requests for information, one finger at a time. They eventually settled on Montevideo, with our arrival there planned towards the end of June.

Although Klaus had calculated that the *Sudur Havid* could probably make it to Montevideo without more diesel, the *Northern Pride* was running so low that she could not. If we were to stay at sea for a few more weeks, a small top-up would be helpful. Alan decided we should join the *Northern Pride* on the 1400-mile round trip to refuel from a tanker just off the Falkland Islands. A better price could be negotiated from the tanker's owners if both boats filled up at the same time.

The three-day slog to rendezvous with the tanker gave us a break from fishing, and the enigmatic Bjorgvin joined the crew on deck to help mend the lines. Bubbles and Boetie had been all too happy to dismiss him as a 'Paper Captain' but now he was splicing lines as fast as anyone, even though he was missing half a thumb – he had slipped with a circular saw years before, trying to save time on a job at home. I had started to talk more and more with Bjorgvin in the Officers' Mess. From *The Satanic Verses* to the closure of the fur farm he had run, the range of topics we covered was surprising given his awkward grasp of English. Today, on deck, it seemed that parenthood was the subject of choice. Many of my crewmates had young families and a few, including Simon, had wives who were pregnant.

'So tell me, Matt, do you have any children?'

I tried the excuse so commonly given by people of my age: I'm not ready yet. I want to stay flexible – to be free to grasp the next opportunity, wherever that may lead. Bjorgvin stopped splicing for a moment, unconvinced by my argument.

'Ah, there is always a reason to put it off, I think. A house to move to or a job to change, not enough money or not enough time. But then, one day, the children arrive, and you discover that you are ready, and that you were ready all along.'

The boat we were to meet, the *Hai Gong You #302*, was a 'reefer', one of the nomadic tankers that act as fuel stations for the world's mariners. A bitter-sweet triumph of modern cost-cutting and efficiency is that a boat no longer needs to return to port to refuel or even to offload her cargo. Our reefer was waiting just outside the twelve-mile limit of the Falkland Islands' territorial waters.

The *Northern Pride* went first, approaching the long, grey and white tanker from the stern. Looking across at our sister-ship, it was a shock to see how hard the last few months had been on her. She wore almost the same colours as us: red antifouling paint below the waterline, blue paint above, a white superstructure and a white rim to her hull. But this was now discoloured by rust and wear. Dents and gouges revealed the daily assault of ropes, weights and anchors, exposing the old, vulnerable steel below. The shot-blasting action of the wind-borne spray and ice added to the damage, and now rust seeped down the hull in streaks from every porthole, winch and seam. If the *Pride* looked beaten, I knew we would look even worse.

We waited the hours until they had finished, watching at a safe distance. Before the *Northern Pride* headed away, an exchange of goods was required. We were short of lubricant oil, and they needed filters and engine spares. Our two boats came close together, bow to bow, and ropes were thrown to allow the plastic-wrapped bundles of spares and the drum of oil to be pulled across.

This was our first and, unknown to us then, last opportunity to catch sight of the *Northern Pride* at sea. It was a chance to see familiar faces from Cape Town, and check that friends were well. It was also a relief to see another boat, something manmade to remind us that there was a world other than the *Sudur Havid*. In the two months since leaving port, we had only seen two or three other vessels on the fishing grounds, usually glimpsed through binoculars as they sailed by. Magnus snapped a photo of us, lined up along the bow, the boat bobbing gently on the calm sea. I didn't know it then, but this would be the last picture of the *Sudur Havid*.

Exchange of spares completed, the *Northern Pride* turned and opened up her engines, smoke billowing from her stack. They were off to try a different fishing area, south of South Georgia, to follow up rumours of a new hotspot. It was now our turn to bunker fuel. Operations were complicated by the fact that the *Hai*

Gong You #302 was Chinese, and carrying a mostly Korean crew who spoke very little English. This became almost unintelligible once passed through the garbling effect of the radio. The tanker was considerably larger than us, carrying 4000 tonnes of fuel, and we manoeuvred close to receive a line thrown across, followed by the hose for the fuel. Calm waters made the operation easier than it could have been, but Bubbles kept grabbing the radio microphone from Boetie, who couldn't keep a straight face when replying to the Korean crew's attempts at English. This should have been funny but for the fact that the *Hai Gong You #302* weighed at least ten times as much as us, and there's nothing like convulsive laughter to cock up delicate manoeuvring. It was only when the boats came together that we could see just how small, old and rusty the *Sudur Havid* really was.

While the fuel tanks were filled, Klaus and the engineers ran around the boat opening and closing valves, operating transfer pumps and monitoring levels. It wasn't long before one of the tanks was full up and diesel poured from the breather pipe on to the deck, popping off the makeshift overflow bag and soaking Klaus and his boiler suit. With so many feet busying about, every part of every deck of the boat was soon covered in slippery, reeking diesel. Both inside and out, the smell was intense and giddying. Only the bridge escaped uncontaminated.

The Korean crew got their revenge for Boetie's behaviour on the radio with the most important transaction of the day: they offered to trade one box of wine for a bag of fish. Boetie assumed a box would mean a case of twelve bottles, so a twenty-kilo sack of fish worth hundreds of pounds was swung across to the tanker. The one-litre carton that came back did not really qualify as a box, to Boetie's eyes. The contents did not really qualify as wine, either, and tasted more like diesel. This was particularly distressing as we had recently discovered that the *Sudur Havid* was running low on liquor. Bubbles had opened one of the last boxes in his special store up on the bridge to discover that it contained only red wine, not his favoured brandy. It was the most upset I had seen him and Boetie all trip.

We had taken on ninety-two tonnes of diesel – much more than the small top-up we had required – and had offloaded only one sack of toothfish. This meant that we were now carrying over one hundred tonnes of fuel, sixty tonnes of fish and a few tonnes of bait, food, water and kit. The *Sudur Havid* was low in the water.

With our decks now closer to the sea's surface, we would be more prone to taking on water from incoming waves. A heavy load could also affect our ability to return upright after being rolled to one side. Instead of bobbing like a duck, in the way Bubbles had described, the boat could struggle to rebalance after each swell. Almost forty years old, altered again and again from her original design, the *Sudur Havid* was being made to carry a dangerously heavy load.

At nightfall, shortly before we departed, Big Danie and his quiet sidekick, Eugene, stood next to the line hauler catching squid with a hand-line. I'd never seen live squid and was curious to know how they were brought aboard with fluorescent lures bristling with sharp hooks. Eugene dropped the lure over the side of the boat and let the line from the spool run freely through his fingers before retrieving it, slowly jigging his hand up and down.

I expected instant results but, of course, the squid were not co-operating. Danie changed his lure, and tried to bite off the excess nylon line next to the knot. He picked up a knife to cut through it instead, pausing in thought as his eyes rested on the blade.

'If this boat ever gets into trouble, Matt, you'll have to watch yourself, eh?'

I thought I had misheard him. Danie had offered me guidance before, but nothing as grave as this. I asked him what he meant.

'I've heard some of the crew talking. If we ever have to get off, if she sinks, they say people will fight with knives.'

This was at odds with my expectations. In an emergency, I assumed that we would pull together – that we would help each other. The idea that I would come to harm not because the ship had sunk, but due to the violence of a crewmate, was horrific.

Eugene nodded.

'I think some people would stab you in the water for a place on a raft.'

'Watch your knives,' Danie instructed. 'Make sure no one takes them.'

He dropped the new rubber lure into the water, and paid out the line. It was an uncomfortable conversation, but I couldn't ignore Danie's advice. They carried on bouncing their squid lines, waiting for the tug that would signal a catch. When the boat lightly rolled, hardly moving at all, Danie pointed to water swilling around under the floor grille, beneath his feet.

'That doesn't normally happen. There's not normally water there.'

Back on the fishing grounds, motivated after the short break, a succession of three- and even 3½-tonne days put another twenty tonnes in the hold. With just ten days' worth of bait left, Joaquim estimated there was room for thirty tonnes more of catch, which meant we would be heading for Montevideo soon. Similar thoughts were running through everyone's heads. After weeks of disappointing hauls, we were thrilled at the prospect of putting into the halfway landing with a boat full of fish. The *Northern Pride*, now fishing over a hundred miles away and plagued by killer whales, would be joining us – her fishing had been going appallingly, but she was in need of supplies and repairs. I was also relieved because I'd finally received a fax from Corinne. I had been sending increasingly desperate faxes and, after three weeks without a reply, was sure she had already gone off with someone else. Fortunately, the secretary in Cape Town had only forgotten to relay the messages on to the boat.

Hi Matt, I am alive and well! I have been writing to you, but it is obviously not reaching you. So I will keep it short and sweet in the hope that it will get to you. I have received your faxes, it is always great to hear from you. Please don't lose heart, I am still thinking of you and missing you every day! Loads of love, Corinne

At daybreak on 3 June, I watched from the wheelhouse as Hannes and Trevor knocked ice off the railings and deck fixtures with mallets. The bitter chill and spray from the night before had caused a thick layer to build up. Too much ice, high up on the ship, could make her dangerously top-heavy.

Later that morning I wandered out on deck for a breather and was watching over the edge of the boat, chatting to Hannes as he gaffed the fish aboard. A drowned bird came up on the line, its feathers sodden, its large body sagging on the hook. Carlos, working at the line hauler and oblivious to my presence, adeptly unhooked the carcass and dropped it into the sea.

I was seething. Were they taking me for a fool? I wasn't surprised that the boat was catching the occasional bird, but they should have let me identify the species. I tried to seem casual as I mentioned the incident to Joaquim in the mess. In our time at sea, I had seen only a few dead petrels hauled aboard. I attempted to visualize the bedraggled corpse, and work out whether I could identify the bird from such a brief glimpse. Laying the identification charts on the table, I ran my finger across them. The pictures all looked the same, but one word stood out. One name, with all its connotations, was impossible to ignore. Everyone knows that it's bad luck to kill an albatross.

TROUBLE

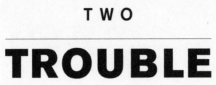

9

SATURDAY, 6 JUNE 1998

At 10:00 I was standing on the main deck of the *Sudur Havid*, look-ing up at the waves. They were big enough to be casting shadows on the deck, blocking out the sun in the middle of the morning. I knew we were fishing a long way from the Equator, and it was winter – so the sun should be low – but something didn't seem right when the waves were casting shadows.

Although huge, the swells were not particularly steep-faced – only a few were forming into the breaking giants that could make work on deck even more dangerous. I reasoned that the strong wind was probably helping us by tearing the peaks down, rather than forcing them into crests. The surface of the sea was streaked in foam and spray. I tried to remember what the crew had been showing me about the wind creating one set of waves (chops) sep-arate from the large oceanic swells. While the swells rumbled through regularly and from one direction, the wind-driven chops came at a different angle, which made for a chaotic seascape. These were the worst conditions we had experienced on the trip so far and the crew were struggling to stay upright. Still, work was to continue as usual.

Earlier that morning I had dressed in full kit: thermals, three pairs of socks, jeans, woolly jumper, padded freezer trousers and waist-coat, hat and deck-suit. Staggering along the bucking deck at 07:30, I yelled my greetings to the deckhands as I passed. Sven was scurry-ing around obsessed with ropes as usual, Trevor was gaffing in his shiny orange gloves and Walu Walu was working at the big winch.

Bracing myself into a corner in the railings above Joaquim, who was on the line hauler, I laughed with Trevor at the conditions we were expected to work in. The boat was rolling and pitching like a rodeo bull. She climbed up each swell and then tipped at the crest before plunging down into the trough. Now and then she punched through breaking waves only to drop alarmingly through the air and land with a dull thud, making the whole hull shudder.

With a foot against a bracket and my back against the railing, I made myself as comfortable as I could and settled in for an hour's shift. The drone of the winches, the hum of the engine, the curses of the fishermen, the hungry whines and chattering of the sea-birds, the banshee howling of the wind and the crashing of the waves on the bow and across the deck: all was muffled by the thick woolly hat pulled down over my ears, and the big hood of my deck-suit pulled up against the saltwater onslaught.

I made a note of the conditions for my daily logbook. The westerly wind was pinning my hood hard against the back of my head so it was a Force 7, maybe an 8, on the Beaufort scale. This was classed as a 'near-gale' or 'fresh gale'. With about a ten-metre swell height, we were disappearing into the troughs while the crests were towering well above the height of the bridge. The visibility was surprisingly good, given the spray from the sea and the sleet showers. Klaus had told me that the cooling water for the engine was currently coming in at − 1°C, the coldest it had been on our trip, and near to the freezing point of seawater.

Two hundred miles away, at King Edward Point on South Georgia, at about this time, the land-based weather station recorded an air temperature of 4°C, and only twenty-five knots of south-easterly wind. The air pressure had fallen to 972.7 millibars from 992.5 the day before. A deep depression, or polar low, was moving through. Cold air from Antarctica rushing north across comparatively warmer water would rise, causing instability in the atmosphere. This would mean severe stormy weather, heavy precipitation and strong winds for those out at sea.

Normally, with my arm shoved up inside a large clear polythene bag, I could write on my clipboard without soaking the paper. My system of bags and knots had worked every day, until now. I was being pounded so hard by waves and spray that the water was forcing its way in and soaking my notes. I carried on recording the catch – toothfish, ray, toothfish, empty hook – trying to concentrate on my task and to ignore the conditions, but it was impossible. I watched in amazement as the lives of my new friends were played out on deck around me. Reaching the crest of each wave, the boat slowly toppled forward before gliding down the face of the swell, as if we were a surfer dropping in. At the bottom of the deepest troughs the bow dug into the oncoming swell, forced deep underwater. The pause while we waited for the bow to clear the surface was heart-stopping. What if she didn't come back up? I couldn't turn to check, as I would get drenched. What if the next one hit us before the boat was ready?

The bow always came back up, water cascading from the decks in time for us to be launched from the crest of the next wave. The water sweeping across the deck caused a melee of staggering and grabbing from the deckhands. Those nearest the bow were swept off balance first, followed by those amidships, before finally the water headed for the alley between the boxes at the stern.

When we were not quite head-on into the waves, I could watch their progress along the side of the ship. They crashed through the railings and bounced off the superstructure, sending up fountains of spray. The biggest swells seemed to move along the deck unbroken – green water, as it is known. Still formed as waves, they hit me on the back, and pushed me into the railings. I had to tense my body to take the blow. Trevor, across the landing hatch from me, got the same wall of water in his face, up his sleeves and down his neck. The icy water forced its way inside his oilskins, and only the exertion of gaffing kept him warm. While I was only scheduled to be out on deck for an hour or so, he was looking at a whole day of this. It was a good job he had had some whisky in his coffee in the morning.

It was even worse for Joaquim, in the pit below me. He was closer to the waterline, facing astern, and the hull blocked any view of oncoming swells. Sorting out a tangle of line in the machine, he failed to see a large swell as it came in. I looked on, idly waiting for the next hook to come aboard. The wave hit the side of the boat and engulfed the pit, submerging Joaquim wholly underwater. He disappeared into the ice-cold deluge and emerged, gasping for breath, as it quickly drained away. Once he had taken a lungful of air, he roared with shock, followed quickly with a tirade of Portuguese curses.

Sven, meanwhile, had been out on deck since first light. For the first time during the trip, Boetie had asked the crew to close the starboard door to the accommodation area, rather than leave it open. This was a precaution in rough seas as the door was exposed to the worst of the weather and could easily be hit by an exceptional wave.

Getting ready to retrieve the buoys, Sven had stepped out on to the front deck next to the inflatable boat. The metal was slick with ice and hydraulic fluid leaking from the main winch. He heard the squeal of his rubber boot as it slid across the oily steel. He hit the railings and almost fell through the gap into the sea below. Hannes' quick reactions saved him – he grabbed Sven by the collar and hauled him to his feet.

There was no time for breakfast, just a mug of coffee laced with brandy brought out by Gideon. Hannes had also been swept off his feet earlier in the morning, carried across the deck by a wash of water. The coffee erased the taste of seawater from Sven's mouth, but it had been a bad start to the day.

Conditions were so rough that it was only possible for him to work when wedged against a railing or in a box, hauling the rope metre by metre, hand over hand. Standing up in the rope boxes, he was clear of the waves washing along the deck, but still exposed to the occasional showers of sleet and snow that passed through. He had a good view of the swells and the wind chop – the waves were forming lips and breaking. Jamming his legs against the wooden walls of the boxes, Sven pulled in the ropes and coiled them neatly, ready for shoot away. He remembered the bad-weather bird he had found weeks before, lying on the rope boxes, and how Hannes had shouted at him: 'They're bad luck, man, throw it overboard!'

Sven didn't blame the storm petrel, but the bad weather had certainly arrived.

My second period of observation out on deck felt like a game, trying to keep up with the fishermen. They had no choice about the conditions they had to work in, so how could I refuse to endure the weather for an hour? Weaving my way around the crew, I heard Boetie's voice rang out over the loudspeaker, in Afrikaans. Trevor translated.

'He says, "Great, now we won't catch any more fish!"'

Despite the curse of having me on duty, not to mention the weather, a steady stream of fish was coming up on the line. They were of a decent size, too. There were lots of the 10–15kg specimens that, once headed and gutted, would still be as big as a man's thigh. Trevor was working hard, heaving them aboard with the gaff.

The thud of the bow hitting the face of a large swell was the warning signal that I would be pelted across my back with icy water a second later. I made sure not to turn around: I could see it all in Trevor's face anyway. When a big wave was coming, his eyes widened before he flinched and grabbed for the rail.

I was glad to step out of the assault from the wind and waves at the end of my shift. With my deck-suit off, I peered tentatively out of the door for oncoming waves, and then timed my run out and up the stairs to the port side of the engine casing, just behind the bridge. This detour would pay off later in the day, as I could hang my deck-suit up next to the exhausts, between the rows of the crew's grubby gloves. It would be warm and dry for my evening observations, when we set the line. As I left the warmth of the engine casing, I made sure to tighten the dogs to seal the massive waterproof door tight.

In the bridge I found Boetie sitting in his chair on the starboard side. To keep still as the boat pitched and rolled he kept his elbows locked against the arms of the chair and his feet resting up against the wood underneath the window.

'How's it, Matt?'

Without taking his eyes off the fishing line coming over the side of the boat, he added, 'Are you enjoying the weather today? A bit choppy, eh?'

Unusually, Bubbles was awake and upright. It was too rough for slumbering on the day bunk and he stood gazing out of the window, or pacing as much as the swell would allow. He rumbled out a greeting in between puffs on his Texan Plain. Standing next to him at the window, I could hear his laboured breathing. He was restless and frowning more than usual.

The radar display was peppered all over with small marks. These were the peaks of the waves appearing as temporary objects before disappearing when the screen refreshed itself. I knew we could adjust the sensitivity of the radar to screen them out, but with waves this big we might miss something important.

From port to starboard, the front of the bridge was a sweep of carefully angled toughened glass. Safe behind this screen, elevated a few metres above the deck, I could look straight into the worst of the conditions. The panorama was spectacular. We were surrounded by monstrous swells, each eight to ten metres in height, which were themselves being shredded by the wind. There was no break in the weather ahead. Reaching the trough of a wave, a fortress of water reared up to fill our view and the bow disappeared.

We hovered in limbo for a few seconds in the white water, before buoyancy won out and the white bow re-emerged, defiant.

I remembered the night I had found Hannes and his friends surfing on the wheelhouse roof, in the Roaring Forties. Then, it was fun. We were bored and the unladen boat moved freely. Now the long-line acted as a fixed point, tethering us to the seabed below, and the boat felt out of time with the sea. We could change the direction in which we were facing, swivelling around the rope, but we could not dodge between the waves. Playtime was over. Hannes and Sven had both had close calls today, and the full force of the cold Southern Ocean was starting to show itself.

10

14:00

I climbed down the stairs and over the threshold of the storm door into the factory. Two hours of sampling work lay ahead of me but the rough weather would make work treacherous. Stephan was squeezed in behind the pot-makers' bench next to Eugene and a row of Ovambo guys, all working with ungloved fingers to untangle and re-coil the lines. Each crew member was braced at his station. With their feet pressed against the rusted table legs and walls, thighs jammed against bright stainless steel wash tanks and worktops, only their upper bodies moved. They swayed in unison with the rolling and jarring of the boat. Melvin, the electrician, had the starboard pump in pieces on the end of the pot-makers' bench. It was playing up again, and he was trying to wire up a replacement.

With no window to the outside world, there was no horizon to provide us with a fixed point of orientation. We depended on our sense of balance and the timing of the swells to determine which way the boat was moving. This was crucial in knowing when to walk and when to wait; when to grab a slippery twenty-kilo fish to take to the freezer, or when to hold on. If we moved carelessly, we could be flung into a girder, a knife or a spinning winch. Big Danie had told me never to walk *down* a sloping deck but to wait, swaying, until I had to climb. In this way, I could control my speed and not be thrown off my feet.

Hannes laughed at me as I staggered into the factory, my hands grabbing for the nearest holds.

'Ha ha, the Observer's gonna get wet today!' A grin split his face from ear to ear at the prospect of seeing me in discomfort.

'Hannes, I'm going to *moer* [beat] you! *Voetsek!* [get lost]' There was no way I was going to punch him, but I wanted to keep the mood friendly.

I arranged my knives, clipboard and measuring tools on top of the large metal hatch that led down to the hold. This was a flat surface that I could work on without getting in the way of the crew. Today, for the first time, Mark had moved to work here too as the waves were hitting the line-hauling pit and exploding through the fish chute. He looked even more pissed off than usual.

'Matt, how are we supposed to work in this? I'm soaked through.'

He severed the head of a toothfish and threw it into a crate. There were hundreds of heads now in the holding area, a sign that we were clearly catching well. Mark reached up for a sharpening steel that was jammed in the rafters and passed it over to me. With a few quick strokes I started putting an edge on my butcher's knife but a wave unexpectedly burst through the fish chute with a whump so loud, I jumped. The spray hit the lights on the ceiling and ran down the back of my neck.

During a normal shift, I could be waiting around for the first thirty fish to arrive. Today the fish were coming fast but, due to their large size and the rocking of the boat, it was all I could do to keep them still enough to be measured. At my feet, a clear icy flow washed from side to side, chattering noisily as it tumbled across the ridges of the steel treadplate deck. This should have been draining away through the scuppers in the side of the hull, or cleared by the pumps. But there was now so much seawater running back and forth that it was confusing my senses. I could see movement out of the corner of my eye, even though I knew I was standing still.

Weighing the fish was another task that was usually simple, as a spring balance was tied to the girder above my head. Two hands were needed to lift the heavier fish up, but today it was difficult to stay upright. With both of my hands grasping the metal meat hook in a toothfish's throat, I strained to raise it to head height. The boat rolled and then jolted as it hit a swell, throwing me off my feet. I missed the scales and fell against Mark.

'Careful! You nearly hooked me!'

I mumbled an embarrassed apology as he helped me back up.

'It's all right. Just don't do that with a knife in your hand.' He moved around the hatch, to give me more room.

On the end of the pot-makers' bench, Melvin continued to struggle to wire up the electric auxiliary pump. It didn't look as large as the pumps that were straining in the wells in the floor, but we hoped that the extra capacity would make up for its shortcomings in size.

By now, even with the access door to the winch pit closed, water was entering through the fish hatch, bucketfuls at a time. If we stopped fishing this instant, we could stop most of the water coming in – but if Boetie wanted to carry on fishing, the hatches would have to remain wide open and exposed to the weather.

A scream came from behind me. I turned to see Grant, his eyes wide with shock, frantically shaking water from inside his oilskins. A large wave had struck the boat and doused him through the line-hatch from head to boot. He cursed as he wiped the seawater from his face. Next to me, water was slopping out of the stainless steel tubs where Big Danie was cleaning the fish. I had never seen this before.

Completing even the simplest of tasks was becoming farcical. There was no way to fasten down my kit on top of the hatch, and when the boat lurched and the water poured through the hatch, it washed away my tools. The delicate butchery required to dissect the toothfish's otoliths, which are the tiny bones suspended in gel around their brains, became more challenging as the twenty-kilo fish slid around. With my finger and thumb in their eyes, the large knife I used to make the horizontal incisions through their skulls was disconcertingly close to my knuckles when the boat jerked. Even worse, many of the fish weren't dead, flicking their tails in a final violent protest as my knife dug into their skin. Combined with the motion of the boat, this sent them off on a slimy pirouette around my workbench. I fought to keep hold of them and not to cut myself with my knife. Once the sharp blade had slipped through the soft bone above their eyes, their struggles stopped and I could flip open the skull and remove the two almond-shaped otoliths with forceps. Meanwhile, all around me the water deepened.

Sven and the crew on deck were having their own problems. At the trough of each ten-metre-high swell, waves crashed on to the boat and washed along the gangway, jumbling up the fishing lines where they were stacked. When the rope tangled, Sven climbed out of his crate and moved forward to free the knot. Gripping the rail tightly, first with one hand, and then the other, he slowly swung his way along the deck, ducking his head to avoid the worst of the spray that lashed across. As he lifted the piled rope, the boat dropped suddenly to starboard.

'Hold on, Sven!' cried Trevor, but the warning came too late and a surge of water swept him off balance and on to the guard-rail. Clinging to the pitted metal, he stared down into the brutal swells, eyeing up his fate. In such a rough sea, he would be pounded deep under the waves or swept out of reach in moments. With the rope running free again, he climbed back into the crate and wedged his foot as deep as he could under the damp coils. It was simply too dangerous to move freely around on deck.

Riding the relentless swells, the boat sometimes dropped away so steeply that Sven could see over the wheelhouse as the bow plunged downwards. He faced directly into the next swell – a giant mass of swirling grey and white, hundreds of tonnes of pressure building behind it. These were moving walls of water, foam-streaked with spray tumbling from their crests.

Sven had given up hoping for an improvement in the conditions: the waves were just as big and the wind just as strong; the clouds seemed darker and more menacing. If there was a choice, he would stop fishing and wait for the weather to calm, but he knew that if he said to the Skipper, 'Listen here, I don't want to work today', he'd be told to fuck off.

At the start of my factory observation period, just a few inches of clean icy water swilled from one side of the factory to the other. Now, a murky grey torrent poured around the hatches and benches. It washed around the tubs of waste, knocking out guts and tails and purging small fragments from all the grubby corners of the factory. Silver sardine scales joined the flow, swept from the boxes of bait defrosting on the floor. Little Danie cleared as much debris as he could from around the pumps, but the water was building up. The noise of the cascade was drowning out all else.

Water passed over my feet with each roll of the hull, but as it backed up around the hatch it got so deep that it went over the top of my boot and flooded inside. I looked down at my foot and realized what had happened. The water was freezing, even after soaking through three pairs of socks.

'That's it!' I declared. 'I'm not working any more.'

I climbed up on to the hatch to escape the water, and sat on the edge of a tub. Looking around at my crewmates I tried to gauge how worried I should be, but no one was panicking. Mark and Alfie continued to head and clean the fish. Joaquim even used his video camera to record the water so that he could show his family the conditions when we got back. With all the experienced mariners on board, surely it wouldn't take long to fix the pumps, and for the water levels to recede?

11

15:00

Joaquim and Carlos climbed up the stairs to the bridge. They had each been up to complain before, separately, but the situation in the factory was now at crisis point. Charlie Baron, the Cape Coloured Bosun, was in close pursuit. These weren't the sort of men to cry wolf – in charge of the deck and the factory, it was in their interest to keep fishing. Together, they might be listened to.

Bubbles and Boetie ignored their pleas. From their own vantage point, high on the bridge, the sea looked no rougher than conditions they had experienced a hundred times before.

'Other boats are still fishing,' Bubbles growled. 'You don't hear them complaining.'

But he was wrong. Of the eleven vessels around South Georgia, only one other boat was still hauling line; the rest had sought shelter or were riding out the storm.

Despite the repeated calls to stop, our winches pulled and the fish came aboard. The waves drenched the crew on deck and in the factory. Melvin gave up trying to wire the new auxiliary pump and returned to his cabin to change into drier clothes.

Joaquim bustled back through the factory, annoyed and complaining loudly. 'Boetie wants to keep fishing. He says we're nearly at the end of the line.'

He pointed angrily to an emergency fire pump, mounted on the wall.

'Hannes, Danie, get that down! See if you can start it up!'

Hannes and Big Danie unbolted the pump and set it on the floor by the wash tubs. It looked like a home electricity generator: a rusty metal frame surrounded by a small diesel-powered engine. It was reassuring to know that there was such a standby. Although small, it resembled the equipment used by firemen to relieve flooded homes. I helped Eugene and Little Danie run a hose from the pump across the factory to the storm door, and out on to the wet-deck. *If we can just get this running,* I thought, *we should be out of trouble.*

Hannes yanked on the starter cord. Nothing. He passed it to Big Danie, who pulled even harder. Again, nothing. Mark van Vuuren checked the valves and gauged the fuel level; I held the outlet pipe, ready for action. The pulls on the starter cord grew more frenzied as frustration and worry set in. Little Danie checked that the components were clean and dry – all that an untrained mind could think of – but we were in dire need of an engineer. Melvin was away changing in his cabin, Klaus was asleep off-duty, Glen was in the engine room and Alfius was nowhere to be seen.

Keeping myself busy, I tried to clear the fish guts and scales clogging the pump wells. I reached into the water and scooped out the debris. My gloved hand felt around the metal body of the pump, but I was nervous that my fingers would get caught in the blades of a spinning impeller. I armed myself with a wooden broom handle. Swirling and scooping, my efforts were mostly in vain.

'Danie, go and get the Chief!' I yelled. 'You won't get that pump started.'

Little Danie hobbled to the engine room, his limp aggravated by the cold. The Chief on duty, in this case, was Glen. Danie returned, and shrugged.

'The Chief's busy.'

'Doing what?'

'He says he's checking the engine.'

'That's it.'

I jostled through the Ovambo pot-makers now gathered out-side in the corridor. They could not possibly work in these conditions, but looked unsure of what to do instead. At the top of the engine room ladder I yelled down.

'Glen! We need help in the factory!'

But the noise of the gunning engine was too loud, and my calls brought no response. I couldn't bring myself to go down the lad-der in wet oilskins: we may have been facing catastrophe but rules were rules. I winced. How ridiculous. Returning to the factory, I urged Little Danie to go back down.

'You get the Chief,' he responded. 'He won't listen to me.'

My search for an engineer was interrupted by Charlie Baron. His eyes fixed mine and he spoke in a level voice, as though trying to assure me that he was calm.

'Matt, I've just been up to see Bubbles and Boetie again, but they don't want to know. It might help if they hear what's happen-ing from you.'

It was only a short climb up the two sets of stairs to the bridge, but I felt like I was stepping into unfamiliar territory. I stood awk-wardly at the doorway, again not wanting to step into a room in my factory-wear. Bubbles and Boetie were both staring straight ahead.

'Has Charlie has been up to see you?' I asked.

No reply. It felt as though I had walked in on an argument. Boe-tie rested his chin on his fingers and stared indifferently out of the window as the crew tried to fix another tangle down on the line. Bubbles kept his back to me, his rough hands spread against the metal windowsills and his shoulders stretched against the thick knit of his jumper. There was no way they hadn't heard me.

'You know there's a bit of water in the factory?'

'Yes, Matt,' replied Bubbles, without turning. He scratched at his beard, and reached for the inevitable cigarette. 'Shut the door on your way out.'

I was stunned. What else could I say? Shaken by their complete disregard I climbed back downstairs. How could the most experienced men on the boat just ignore what was going on?

Glen and I hadn't been getting on well lately as cabin-mates. The bonhomie at the start of the trip had been replaced by mutual annoyance, after sharing a small space for so long. I was still nervous about how he would react to my wet gear, but I took a deep breath and lowered myself down the ladder to the engine room. Seeing my boots, he instantly shouted and signalled for me to go back, following me up.

I leant forward to speak into his ear. Even at the top of the ladder, the din from the engine was thunderous.

'We have . . . the diesel pump . . . but can't . . . get it started.'

He stood back and glared at me. I wanted to make it clear that we needed help, but now he looked exasperated.

'We need an engineer . . . It's just Danie the Greaser . . . he doesn't know mechanics.'

'Why are you shouting at me?' he demanded. He turned away, and shinned back down the ladder, shaking his head. I watched as he disappeared back into the warm, dry engine room.

A fear was now rising in me, bubbling under the surface. Could no one else see that the *Sudur Havid* was in peril? Everyone I asked for help seemed unconcerned. I returned to the factory to clear debris from the pump wells. Many of the Ovambo pot-makers had left, fed up with the water flooding their workbenches. The deckhands were still gathered around the diesel pump, trying to start it. Big Danie called out across the room.

'Hey, Engelsman, can I borrow one of your knives?'

I climbed over the hatch and reached down for my tools. Water poured through the fish chute next to me, spraying the back of my neck and filling the air with saltwater mist. Selecting a razor-sharp filleting knife, I passed it to him, handle first. Instead of using it to fix the pump, he turned the glinting blade and stabbed it hard into the wooden cutting block in the middle of the room. He took his hat off and held it in his hands; he was hot from the exertion of pulling on the starter cord. The knife stood upright, waiting.

'There, now it is ready!'

He caught my eye, and I understood. Like a flag, the knife stood between us as an eight-inch stainless steel signal that, in Danie's opinion, things were about to get much more serious.

I picked up my two remaining knives. With its twelve-inch blade honed like a scalpel, the butcher's knife was unwieldy. The other knife was small and sharp-pointed. It would be more practical for self-defence, and safer to conceal. I could even tuck it into my oil-skins. But I stopped myself. What was I thinking? How could I stoop to fight a crewmate for a place in a raft? If I pulled a knife on anyone, surely it could only end in injury for myself? I put them both back in their rack. There was no way I would be able to fight like that.

Being an outsider, I had always avoided ordering the crew around. Now, the time for diplomacy was over. In the crew's mess I found Alfius drinking coffee and Melvin sitting idly next to him.

'We really need your help with the diesel pump.'

'Oh no, no. I'm not on duty,' responded Alfius, staring into his mug.

'I don't have any boots!' said Melvin.

I grabbed a pair close to him and thrust them into his hands.

'Put them on, now!' When he still refused to move I dragged him by the arm into the factory. He tried to climb along the benches to keep dry as the alleyway was now thigh-deep in ice-cold seawater. 'Get in the water, now,' I ordered.

Melvin took one look at the pump.

'The only man who knows how to start that is Alfius.'

I turned to see Alfius, finally wading through the corridor in his boiler suit. Bubbles leant through the factory door behind him.

'Where are the Chiefs?' yelled Bubbles, 'Where are the Chiefs?'

'We can't find them.'

The deckhands stood back and we watched Alfius with hope. Of all the men aboard, he was the most familiar with the *Sudur Havid*'s equipment and its quirks. This pump could save us. He made a few attempts to start it up, yanking on the starter cord and checking the fuel and valves. Nothing.

He mumbled something into his beard, then left the factory again. 'Where's he gone?' asked Big Danie.

'Maybe he needs some tools,' Hannes suggested. We had all been hoping to hear the noisy cough and rattle of a diesel engine. The silence was gutting. After all the hassle to get Alfius into the factory, he had disappeared again in under two minutes. I left them, determined to find a Chief Engineer.

Torn from his sleep, Klaus had walked into mayhem. A cable had now been strung across the factory, to provide power for the auxiliary pump to starboard, and he was attempting to help Glen attach the new cable to the supply fuse box. Two engineers, with sixty years of experience between them, to wire up a single connection.

'Klaus, we can't start the diesel pump in the factory.'

He turned his attention from the wires in his hand, and looked over his glasses at me.

'I'm trying to sort out, you know, trying to sort this out.' He stumbled over his English.

Instead, Klaus was called up to the bridge. Boetie ordered him to start pumping fuel from the starboard to the port tank, in an attempt to re-balance the ship. This was ludicrous, complained Klaus. Even at full capacity, the pumps could only move eight tonnes an hour. We didn't have an hour.

I heard Bubbles call down from the bridge above.

'Shut off the hydraulics!'

Glen dropped down the ladder into the engine room. The power for the deck winches and the line hauler was cut. Finally, after hours of taking on water, we stopped fishing. I scrambled back over the half storm door and made my way along the swirling corridor into the factory.

Out on deck, the rope stopped coming aboard just as Joaquim emerged from the factory. This gave Sven a chance for a cigarette. With damp hands and no shelter from the wind it was a struggle to get it to light. He braced his legs among the rope coils and sat back on the edge of the wooden crate. Joaquim was yelling up at Boetie, who was leaning out from the door of the wheelhouse above. Even with the scream of the wind and the pounding of the waves, Joaquim's booming voice could be heard back at the boxes loudly enough for Sven to catch the gist of the conversation. Joaquim was complaining that the factory deck was flooded, and that they should cut the line. Bubbles wanted to do this, but Boetie wanted to press on. The line was nearly in – only a kilometre left – and we would be finished soon. Now that he had a chance to stop and fully observe what was going on, Sven could see that the boat's motion was troubled, and that we were rolling more deeply to starboard.

Joaquim crossed the deck and put his knife to the thick rope, close to the winch. Under such tension, it didn't take much to sever the line. The free end whipped over the roller and slashed into the water. On the few occasions they had cut the line before, Joaquim had always tied on marker buoys first. Sven watched as the end of the rope disappeared into the water, with no buoys attached.

The *Sudur Havid* wallowed now, low in the water. The waves hit higher on the starboard side of the boat, which meant that more water entered the hatch. Worse still, there was now so much water washing around, and the motion of the boat was so severe, that the waste bins were knocked over. Hundreds of kilograms of guts, tails and scales were added to the debris swilling around.

The fluorescent strip lights in the factory started to fuse, overwhelmed by the saltwater and spray. Some had gone out, a few flickered ominously. Their cold flashes illuminated the grey water gushing around. I looked at the mess. Of the thirty-eight people aboard, only eight of us were left in the factory. Where had everyone else gone? What more pressing tasks could they have to do? Only the deckhands and I remained there.

Glen finally appeared, clad in short wellington boots and oilskin trousers. Elastic bands were fastened neatly around his trouser legs to seal the water out. I tried to explain hastily what was wrong.

'The starboard pump is down, Melvin can't get the auxiliary started, the port pump is blocked and these guys can't get the diesel pump going.'

Glen squeezed the discharge tube leading overboard from the port pump but it was soft. Next, he knelt and reached deep into the well, bringing up a fistful of debris. But a wave rolled us to port, and Glen was plunged underwater. A torrent of freezing saltwater engulfed his lean frame, and he disappeared. I reached down to grab the collar of his jacket, and lifted him on to his feet. He was drenched, gasping and spluttering.

'What do I do?' I asked. 'Tell me what to do.'

'There's a metal sieve near the bottom of the pump. Scrape it with your hands. You'll know when it's working again. The discharge tube will go hard.'

If only I had known this earlier. For all my efforts with the broom handle, I hadn't known there was a grille to clear, and that it was safe to reach right in. I plunged my arm deep in the water and found the metal latticework with my fingers. I tried to scrape it clean, but this was only feasible when we rolled to starboard;

with the boat to port, the sieve disappeared out of my reach under-water. I crouched, waiting for the water to move away as we rolled back. The discharge tube was still soft – my effort was not having any effect – but then, one more scrape and the tube hardened. I watched the water level in the well drop, and congratulated myself. We now had one working pump.

At this precise moment, as I was on my knees, a tipping point was reached and passed. Unannounced, unacknowledged, but apparent to all of us just minutes later. The boat had been taking on more water than she could drain for some time but now the process had accelerated.

Click. A light suddenly went on in my mind. I was no longer getting wet, the well was not being refilled. For once, the water hadn't come back over to port. I looked over with dread at the star-board side of the factory, which was now six feet deep in grey murk. The water almost reached the ceiling, and the weight pinned the *Sudur Havid* down.

A bird's eye would see through the spray that she now lay with her heavy bow low in the water, and her stern slightly raised. She leant heavily, with her port side twelve feet up in the air and her starboard rail down in the sea. Waves broke over her and ran down her decks. The boat was no longer rolling, she was listing.

12

15:40

The weight of the water pulled the *Sudur Havid* down so that we hung there, like a boxer on the ropes, being pummelled by the giant waves. Bubbles and Boetie battled to keep the bow into the swells but it was impossible. Any deviation from a head-on course was punished, exposing the vulnerable starboard hatches to the full force of the sea. If the boat was caught side-on to the swells we would surely capsize.

Below deck, the factory was dark and oppressive. Many of the lights had fused or were flickering, and the familiar banter of work had been replaced by the deep groaning of the hull and the thunderous crashing of waves. The right-hand side of the room was completely submerged and water reached the ceiling as the boat swayed to starboard, before ebbing down the wall as we rolled back towards level.

A wave hit the boat. With a sound like a gunshot, the storm door burst inward. Morné and Big Danie waded in to push the door closed. As the boat rolled a little to port, and the flow lessened, they seized their chance and the door slammed shut. Morné turned the dogs, the levers that locked the door, but they would not catch. The gunshot had been the failure of two of the thick metal levers. Another wave. Morné and Danie were powerless to keep the door closed against the flow. There was now no barrier to the ingress of water.

I stood up from the pump, turning to see a flurry of bright-orange shapes dancing across the factory. Unable to get into the locked cup-board, Sven and Hannes had smashed the padlock off with an axe. Armfuls of lifejackets were thrown down the stairs and along a chain of hands. Little Danie passed a few to Mark and Brian, who pulled them over their heads. They were of a familiar design: large blocks of foam on the shoulders and chest for buoyancy, with long ties to secure them in place once donned. There were not enough lifejackets passed down for Glen and me but it was time to leave. Nothing more could be done in the factory.

I didn't know if we would be abandoning the boat, or if there was a plan to save her. One thing was clear. I didn't want to be in an enclosed factory if the boat capsized or sank. If I wanted a life-jacket, I would have to find one for myself.

I left Morné, Hannes and Big Danie to their last-ditch efforts. The only escape route was down the corridor to starboard, but this was now deeply flooded. After so long kneeling and wading in the ice-cold water, the plunge in up to my waist came as no shock. The surge of adrenaline helped. I hardly noticed how cold the water felt.

I clambered up on to the pot-makers' bench, my fingers grip-ping the girders above for support. Edging along the slanted metalwork top behind Glen, our heads brushed the ceiling. The water below was a tangle of snares: tubs of line and hooks floated insidiously, ropes looped and uncoiled just under the water's sur-face and wires dangled from Melvin's unfinished cabling. I flinched as the shorting lights sparked and spluttered so close to my face. Grabbing the top of the doorway with both hands, I dropped down off the bench and stepped over the threshold of the storm door.

After the chaos of the flooded factory, the dry corridor of the crew area was eerily serene. That was, if you could ignore the absurd angle at which it was now poised, and the jumble of boots, towels and jackets that had fallen on to the floor. Two pot-makers shambled past, on their way upstairs from their cabins. Grunter leant against the galley doorway, with a cloth over his shoulder, looking only vaguely puzzled as though he were watching someone else making a mess.

Mark and I examined the lower half of the factory door, debating whether to fasten it or to leave it open. Once a waterproof storm door, it had been cut horizontally in half with a blowtorch years before, wrecking its integrity but allowing coffee and commands to be passed through the top hatch in rough weather. With people still in the factory, the whole door could not be shut.

'Leave both hatches open, Matt. It will let the water level out a bit.'

'No, we should close the bottom and keep the water in the factory. It will buy us some time. An engineer might be back in a minute with a pump.'

Morné shouldered by, one of the last to leave the factory. Hearing cries from inside, I looked through to see Hannes cutting Big Danie free from a tangle of hooks and lines. They squeezed past too, and we closed the lower half of the door, locking it as best we could.

I followed Mark to the upper deck. Grabbing the handrail to pull myself up the stairs, I was surprised at how easy it was to ascend. The slant of the boat made the stairs less steep, a welcome aid in the struggle to escape.

The corridor at the top was strewn with more lifejackets. I grabbed one on my way up the sloping corridor past my cabin and headed out through the door on the port side.

The deck was crowded with deckhands and pot-makers, all scrambling to pull on their lifejackets.

'What's happening?' I asked Trevor, almost flippantly. 'Are we abandoning ship or what?'

'Yes, Matt,' he replied, matter-of-fact.

Hearing it so bluntly, I was taken aback. I thought of my previous trips on research boats. Abandon ship should be announced by a signal on the ship's whistles, or a call over loudspeakers. I still thought, somehow, that the crisis was going to be averted at the last moment. There had to be something more that could be done to save the ship?

Peinge appeared at the door next to Morné and me. He was carrying a large sports holdall across his chest.

'Where the hell do you think you're going?' asked Hannes.

'I'm going home!'

My time below deck had obscured the hellish view. Huge swells were being torn apart by the wind on all sides of us as far out as I could see. The horizon confirmed we were now 30° from level.

I looked around at Klaus, Glen, Alfius and Melvin. All of the trained engineers were on deck. If they were on deck and everyone was out of the factory, then there was no way back. There was no one below to save the boat.

Oh my God, we are actually abandoning. Breathing heavily, I tried to calm myself. I ducked back through the door and into my cabin, but my most-familiar space was now alien. Coats and curtains hung clear of the walls and clothes had fallen to the floor.

I needed to consider strategy for a moment. While we had been in the factory, trying to save the *Sudur Havid*, the rest of the crew had assembled on deck and were now dressed and ready. If they made a move to abandon ship in the next few minutes, I would be left behind. I had to get myself prepared. Quickly.

There was no time to think of possessions, not that I had anything with me of value. But my flotation suit wasn't in my cabin. After the drenched morning on deck, I had hung it in the chimney stack to dry. A dark thought struck me. Danie said the crew would fight for a place in a life-raft. What would they do for a flotation suit that could save their lives? They had all seen me wearing it, and even referred to it as my survival suit. Would I start a panic if I suddenly appeared with it? No, no, I wouldn't get it. I would take my chances, like the rest of the crew. But what if it offered my only chance of survival?

I walked as casually as I could past the crew, then vaulted up the metal stairs to the heavy door and into the engine casing. Opening the dogs, I slid inside, closing the hatch behind me. I would don the suit discreetly, out of sight. The list of the boat made the dimly lit space claustrophobic and disorientating. The metal grille floor was slippery, and I leant back against the dirty painted wall. The clamour of noise from the engines below and the exhausts added to the claustrophobia. It was difficult to stand, let alone to fit the suit over my factory clothes. I had so many layers, and they bunched up as I rushed. The damp oilskins stuck to the fabric, and I could only get the suit half over my shoulders; the layers of clothes blocked the zip. But I could finish getting dressed outside.

A moment later, my thoughts had a new focus. Why did I close this door? The boat's lean made the metal hatch too heavy to open from the inside, and standing on the sloping floor I couldn't use my full weight against it. Bracing my feet against a girder behind me, I lay my palms flat against the cold steel and strained. It didn't budge.

Maybe one of the dogs had slipped and was now locking me in? I checked them, to make sure, and then pushed at the door again. It was hopeless. I was stuck in a sinking ship. I knew the starboard door was jammed because it had seized up a week before.

Frustration and dread welled up deep inside me. What if I couldn't get out? My chest tightened. Would I go down with the boat because I tried to get my suit?

1. The *Sudur Havid*, then called *Leikur*, not long after her launch in Norway, 1964.
(Photo: unknown)

2. The *Sudur Havid* trawling for prawns off Greenland in 1979. This photo captures her spirit as I remember her.
(Photo: Regin Torkilsson)

3. An iced-up *Sudur Havid* hauling her nets off Greenland in 1979. The stern gantry, which caused us so much trouble, is clearly visible.
(Photo: Regin Torkilsson)

4. With my mum and sister in Somerset before the trip, 1997. I know: bad hair, dreadful beard, but I was young.
(Photo: Chris Lewis)

5. *Top*: The beautiful mountains above Cumberland Bay, South Georgia, in June 1998.
(Photo: Phil Marshall)

6. *Above*: The bow of the *Isla Camila* digs into yet another southern ocean swell.
(Photo: Phil Marshall)

7. *Above left*: The *Isla Sofia* coming up to her sister-ship to exchange spares. This is the view we had of the *Isla Camila*, albeit at night, as she came to rescue us.
(Photo: Phil Marshall)

8. *Above*: Wind-streaked swells make for fun working conditions on the *Isla Camila*.
(Photo: Phil Marshall)

9. *Above right*: Gaffing a toothfish aboard the *Isla Camila*. The thick mainline is in the foreground.
(Photo: Phil Marshall)

10. *Below right*: A good haul of toothfish waiting to be processed on the *Isla Camila*. The white fish on the left probably died when just hooked, rather than once aboard, and has deteriorated.
(Photo: Phil Marshall)

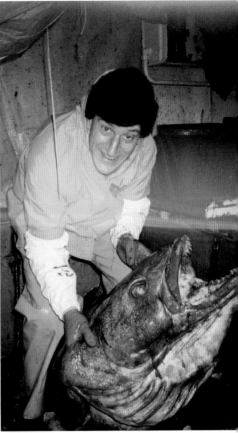

11. *Above left and right*: Phil Marshall with a monster toothfish on the *Isla Camila*.

12. *Left*: Baiting the hooks with sardines, prior to shooting the line, on the *Isla Camila*. Jesus Pousada is on the right. Our line pots were circular.

(Photo: Phil Marshall)

13. *Right*: Rough seas never look as impressive in photos. The work continues regardless on the *Isla Camila*. (Photo: Phil Marshall)

14. *Below*: A black-browed albatross follows the *Isla Camila*, with South Georgia providing a stunning backdrop. (Photo: Phil Marshall)

15. *Right*: A petrel (probably white-chinned) discovers the drawback of longline fishing. This bird was lucky: it was caught as the line was retrieved and could be released, alive, once the hook had been removed. (Photo: Phil Marshall)

16. A sperm whale dives near the *Isla Camila*, probably to steal fish from the line. Giant petrels, wandering albatross and black-browed albatross wait in the hope of a stray morsel. (Photo: Phil Marshall)

17. This picture of the *Ocean Harvest* shows the conditions that the *Sudur Havid* faced. All pictures of the *Sudur Havid* taken by the crew during the trip were lost.
(Photo © Philip Stephen/bluegreenpictures.com)

18. *Below*: The start of the fishing season: Phil with crew of the *Isla Camila*, King Edward Cove, South Georgia, April 1998. Jesus Pousada is in orange.

19. *Right*: Marco, the First Mate, keeps watch on the bridge of the *Isla Camila*, April 1998.
(Photo: Phil Marshall)

20. The *Sudur Havid* waiting to refuel near the Falkland Islands, shot from the *Northern Pride*. I am somewhere near the bow.
(Photo: Magnus Johnson)

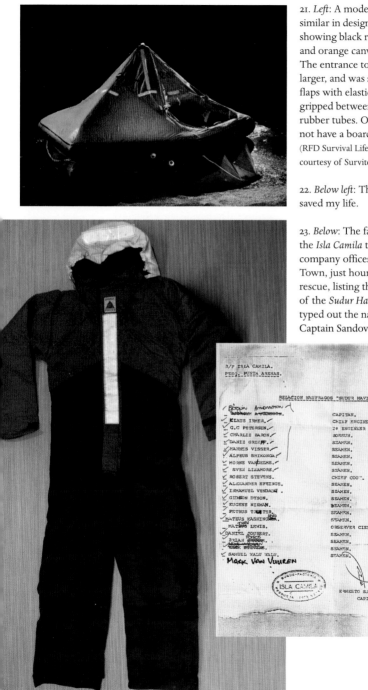

21. *Left*: A modern life-raft, similar in design to ours, showing black rubber tubes and orange canvas canopy. The entrance to our raft was larger, and was sealed by flaps with elastic hems which gripped between the two rubber tubes. Our raft did not have a boarding ramp. (RFD Survival Life-raft: image courtesy of Survitec Group)

22. *Below left*: The suit that saved my life.

23. *Below*: The fax sent from the *Isla Camila* to the company offices in Cape Town, just hours after our rescue, listing the survivors of the *Sudur Havid*. Phil typed out the names and Captain Sandoval signed it.

B/P ISLA CAMILA.
PESQ. PUNTA ARENAS.

RELACION NAUFRAGOS "SUDUR HAVID".

BODUN ARMODASON	CAPITAN.	ICELAND.
KLAUS IRMER.	CHIEF ENGINEER.	GERMAN.
G.C PETERSEN.	2º ENGINEER.	S. AFRICAN.
CHARLIE BARON.	BOSSUN.	S. AFRICAN.
DANIE GREEFF.	SEAMEN.	S. AFRICAN.
HANNES VISSER.	SEAMEN.	S. AFRICAN.
ALPEUS SHIKONGA	SEAMEN.	NAMIBIAN.
MORNE VANDEEMS.	SEAMEN.	S. AFRICAN.
SVEN LIZAMORE.	SEAMEN.	S. AFRICAN.
ROBERT STEVENS.	CHIEF COOK.	S. AFRICAN.
ALEXANDER EPEINGE.	SEAMEN.	S. AFRICAN.
INMAMUEL VENDACU.	SEAMEN.	NAMIBIAN.
GIDEON DYSON.	SEAMEN.	S. AFRICAN.
EUGENE NIEMAN.	SEAMEN.	S. AFRICAN.
PETRUS TRUITER.	SEAMEN.	S. AFRICAN.
MATEUS KASHINGWA. THEN	SEAMEN.	NAMIBIA.
MATEUS LEWIS.	OBSERVER CIENTIFIC.	BRITISH.
DANIEL JOUBERT.	SEAMEN.	S. AFRICAN.
BRIAN BRUCE.	SEAMEN.	S. AFRICAN.
CLEM STEVENS.	SEAMEN.	S. AFRICAN.
SAMUEL WALU WALU.	SEAMEN.	S. AFRICAN.

MARK VAN VUUREN

ISLA CAMILA

ERNESTO SAND VAL A.
CAPITAN.

24. We were glad to get ashore. The boarded-up buildings of a snowy King Edward Point, South Georgia, June 1998. (Photo: Phil Marshall)

25. The memorial service in Grytviken, in borrowed freezer suits and camouflage. It seemed wrong to smile. Bjorgvin and a few others were left at the accommodation block, due to frostbite. (Photo: Phil Marshall)

26. *Left*: Sven, Stephan, Morné and me at the memorial service in Grytviken.
(Photo: Phil Marshall)

27. *Below*: The church in Grytviken, South Georgia.
(Photo: Donald Smith)

28. Memorial cross to those lost on the *Sudur Havid*, on the hill above Grytviken. What a view.
(Photo: Pat Lurcock)

29. *Above*: The *Isla Camila* at anchor in King Edward Cove, South Georgia, June 1998.
(Photo: Phil Marshall)

30. *Right*: Getting our smiles back on the *RFA Gold Rover*: Stephan, Sven, Big Danie, Eugene and me.
(Photo: Phil Marshall)

31. *Left*: Sven, me, Morné and Phil on the *Gold Rover*. We look so young!

32. *Below*: Calm weather and clear skies on our way to the pub, Stanley, Falkland Islands, June 1998.
(Photo: Phil Marshall)

33. *Left*: Big Danie and Hannes get the braai going on the Falkland Islands. Hannes's eye is still swollen from the gaffing mishap. (Photo: Phil Marshall)

34. *Above*: Things were never boring when Hannes was around. Mark, Hannes and Brian: a crew once again. Brian's house, Mitchell's Plain, Cape Town, 1999.

35. The survivors, plus Phil but minus Efeinge, in the Seaman's Mission in Stanley, Falkland Islands. *Back row, left to right*: Charlie, Bjorgvin, Brian, Little Danie, Hannes hugging Klaus, Sven, Eugene, Stephan, Big Danie, Kashingola, Morné, Grunter. *Front row, left to right*: Gideon, Glen (*at table*), Walu Walu, Phil, Vendadu, Alfius, Me, Mark. (Photo: Mike Hughes)

36. *Left*: Life-ring, now placed as a memorial in the church in Grytviken, South Georgia.

37. *Below*: In my favourite deck-suit, ready to go back to sea, Aberdeen, 1999.
(Photo courtesy of Cosalt/ Aberdeen Journals)

38. Three reasons I'm glad I survived: Camila, Corinne and Tate in the river near our home in Scotland, June 2013.

39. Holding an African pygmy hedgehog in my new career as Mr Bug, getting kids interested in wildlife.

40. Thank you.

13

15:45

Out on deck, Stephan watched a dozen of the Ovambo crewmen milling around. There was no purpose in their movements and chatter: it looked as though they were waiting for a bus, not facing an abandon-ship. Grunter and Simon arrived, still wearing their galley clothes of T-shirts, aprons and sandals. They looked out of place, stood among all the oilskins and woolly hats.

Stephan remembered falling overboard while fishing off the coast of South Africa, years before. He had struggled to swim properly in his boots and oilskins, and had sunk so quickly that it had felt like they were dragging him down. If he ended up in the water today, it would be hard enough to swim through the cold chop and swells. He kicked off his boots, peeled off his oilskins and stepped out of his freezer suit for good measure, reasoning that this too would be deadweight in the water. Even on this sheltered side of the boat, Stephan could feel the warmth being stripped from him through the damp layers. He was left in only his socks, jogging bottoms and jumper. The water in South Africa had been crisp and clear but when Stephan looked at the mountainous swells surrounding the boat now, the sea was a dismal steel grey, streaked with spray. He knew it would be bitterly cold.

Just as he was about to put on his own lifejacket, Stephan realized that many of the pot-makers around him had never worn one before. One Namibian man, named Haimbodi, was trying to force his on inside out, and couldn't untangle the ties. Stephan helped him and barked out instructions in Afrikaans to the others.

'Over the head, cross the ties around the back and knot.'

From their faces, it was obvious they didn't comprehend how critical the boat's condition had become.

Sven, meanwhile, was waiting for the boat to roll over and to fully capsize, taking us all with it. With the boat so low in the water and leaning over so far, she could go suddenly.

'Loosen the rubber duck!' yelled Boetie.

Sven edged forward, alongside Big Danie and Hannes, to cut the inflatable dinghy loose and get it over the side. The extreme list of the boat made it impossible to walk normally, so he crouched and shuffled along where the wall of the wheelhouse met the metal deck. Normally two metres above the sea's surface, the main deck was now awash with water. It sloped away into the ocean and the waves crashed upon it like the tide on a beach.

Holding tight to the railings, Big Danie cut the ropes and straps securing the dinghy. When they tried to lift the heavy rubber boat, it became clear that they would be unable to raise it up over the guardrail and into the lee of the ship. They were more likely to lose control of it and to fall into the waves to starboard in the process. The dinghy was left sitting in its cradle.

'At least it will float free when the boat sinks.'

It wasn't the kind of thought that Sven had ever expected to have on this trip. Moving back behind the wheelhouse again, he joined the rest of the crew, and waited for instructions. Like Stephan, he stripped off his boots and oilskins; he would not try to swim in them. Somehow, Sven had managed to hand out all of the lifejackets without leaving one for himself. But there was no time to worry about that now.

★

Inside the engine casing, trapped by the heavy door, I waited for the boat to roll. Timing my effort to push when the boat was closest to upright, I summoned all my strength. The door moved just a little. I pushed harder. It inched open a fraction more. Finally, after waiting for one last roll of the hull, I gave another push. It clanged back against the outside of the funnel, wide open. I flung myself on to the walkway outside, one rubber glove off and my suit still open to the waist.

Catching my breath, I leant against the outside of the chimney. I felt foolish that such a selfish survival mission had nearly led to my own demise; I hoped no one had seen me emerge so agitated. Relief washed over me, then passed as quickly as it had come.

I pulled my lifejacket over my head and groped around to secure the ties. My rubber glove was now jammed in place by my bunched sleeves, making it difficult to manipulate the thin straps. In my haste, I formed scruffy knots and pulled them as tight as I could. I would have to sort them out later.

The deck below was busy with crew: knitted hats, gleaming oilskins and a blur of orange jackets. All was ready to go, it seemed. Compared to the relatively ordered appearance of my crewmates, my hurried preparations had left me looking dishevelled. I had stayed in the factory too long.

Bubbles was standing just a few feet away from me, at the open door to the bridge. He was still wearing just his jumper. Although his brow was furrowed he looked curiously composed, staring down at his men and out at the wind-torn swells. Behind him, I could see Boetie moving around inside the bridge. I assumed he was making preparations.

Between Bubbles and me, two white fibreglass canisters the size of oil drums sat in their cradles. Each contained an inflatable rubber life-raft – one for twelve men, one for twenty. A matching pair sat on the starboard side of the funnel. Once triggered, the gas cylinders inside would inflate the tubes of the rafts in under a minute, shedding the two halves of the capsule. This would produce a circular raft, three or four metres in diameter, with a canopy made from fabric.

My foray into the engine casing had unwittingly put me in the right place to launch the life-rafts, but I didn't have a clue what to do. I thought of the disaster films I had seen. The boat always rolled over and the inflatable life-rafts popped up neatly, bobbing next to the wreck. This relied on the automatic releases activated after the ship had sunk, but we needed the rafts now. Without survival training I was completely unfamiliar with the kit or its operation. I tried to take comfort from the men around me who had spent years at sea. Joaquim climbed up the stairs behind me. Surely he would know what to do?

While Bubbles watched, Joaquim and I released the latches of the webbing strap that held the twenty-man life-raft in its cradle. Joaquim pulled out his knife and cut the plastic wrapping bands around the fibreglass canister. He wasn't sure if we needed to cut them but they were off in a few seconds. I passed the rope painter, the rope tether that would secure the raft, down to Carlos to be tied on to the railings below. Now we were ready to push the first canister off its cradle and into the water, where it would inflate. Due to the boat's tilt, a good shove would be necessary for it to clear the deck below. We looked at Bubbles.

'Ready?'

'Hold on . . .' We waited. Bubbles took a final drag on his cigarette. He flicked away the stub, which pirouetted end over end, out to sea. My eyes followed the tiny fleck of orange as the wind carried it far from the boat. 'Go!'

We pushed hard. The canister rolled out of its cradle and plunged outwards, clearing the deck and the railing. It hit the water cleanly and Carlos yanked on the painter. Nothing. It didn't inflate. Sitting uselessly in its fibreglass casing, it bobbed in the lee of the boat.

Had we done something wrong? Would this happen with all of the rafts? With no time to wait, we raced to release the straps and cut the bands of the next raft, designed to carry twelve men. Once Carlos had tied the painter, Joaquim and I braced ourselves and pushed. Timing our effort badly, the canister left the cradle just as the *Sudur Havid* rolled further to starboard. The heavy container fell on to the deck below with a loud bang, just missing Charlie. The two halves of the casing broke open; we hoped that the raft had not been damaged. Hannes and Brian manhandled it over the side and tugged hard on the painter rope. With a loud hiss, the raft started to inflate. *Thank God*, at least one was working.

'And now the starboard rafts?' I asked.

'I wouldn't bother,' dismissed Bubbles. 'They'll be of no use, better to board these.'

This was madness. Admittedly the starboard vessels were to windward and would be difficult to board, but so far we only had one twelve-man raft for the thirty-eight of us on board. What could be Bubbles' rationale for leaving an escape craft behind on a sinking ship? He turned away, and went back on to the bridge.

Joaquim grabbed me by the shoulder. 'We'll launch them too, Matt.'

He bolted down the stairs and ran around the back of the funnel; I thought it would be quicker to go through the bridge. Bubbles was stowing items into a small black sports bag. I couldn't see what he was packing, but imagined it was at least some flares and a handheld VHF radio. I wasn't going to ask him again, but he didn't try to stop me as I ran to launch the starboard rafts.

Staggering through, I heard frantic voices from the radio blurting *'Isla Sofia, Isla Sofia . . .'* in heavy Spanish accents. It sounded like the voice of Captain Andreas on the *Northern Pride*. The strain told me that they knew we were in trouble. At least a Mayday had been sent.

Leaving the bridge through the starboard door, I noticed the red radio beacons still held in their racks. I knew that we attached radio beacons to the long-line buoys, but we also had emergency radio beacons (EPIRBS) on board. I'd heard that these were the ones on the bridge, and that the rest were stored in float-free cradles on the roof. EPIRBS are buoyant plastic beacons the size of a wine bottle. When activated, they emit a unique signal to alert rescue services of a boat's location. In their racks the beacons were useless, but taken in the rafts, or simply thrown into the water, they could give us a fighting chance of being found. I remembered that the satellite communications system had the ability to send a distress signal, triggered by pressing and holding two grey buttons for a few seconds. If received, the distress signals from either the EPIRB or the satellite system could alert the maritime rescue authorities that we were in need of immediate assistance. Desperate to launch the remaining rafts, I had to trust that our officers in command would do everything in their power to save us.

I met Joaquim again on the walkway, which now hung out over the sea with the list of the boat. Below us, on the unsheltered side of the boat, the waves were pounding against the railings and the sloping deck. When the boat rolled into the troughs between the swells, filling our field of vision, the crests towered many metres above us. The wind filled the air with spray. Mark and Charlie took the rope painters we passed down to them. It took just moments to release the two rafts as we were faster now at freeing the straps and cutting the bands, and the canisters only needed a light push to roll them out of their supports due to the slant to starboard. Hitting the water, the capsules burst open and both rafts began inflating with the reassuring sound of rushing gas and the creaking of unfolding rubber. Once fully blown up, they sat high in the water but were thrown back against the boat by the wind and the sea. Mark and Charlie pulled them along the side of the boat, dragging them by their rope painters to better boarding points at the stern.

I was still clinging to the hope that the *Sudur Havid* would somehow survive, or that another boat would come to our aid. But until such a guardian angel materialized, we had to prepare to board the rafts. Of the four vessels deployed, only three had inflated. With thirty-eight crew on board, I calculated that we would still be OK. Two of the rafts seated twelve men each; the largest could carry twenty. Even without the fourth, that made forty-four safe places.

My descent to the working deck was treacherous. The narrow metal stairway was always steep, but with the boat tilted so far overboard each wet stair was sloping off-camber, and moved as we pitched and rolled. If I fell, it would be on to the metal railings three metres below, or straight into the foaming sea beyond. The seabirds, so abundant whenever we hauled the line, had disappeared. I scrambled down on to the deck, awash with waves, and headed towards the stern.

As I paused for a moment by the funnel, alone for just a few seconds, water swirled over my boots. The gravity of the situation closed in on me. *This could be it, I might not get out of this one.* I fought to get my breathing under control, and to quell the rising panic. Wrenching off my glove I secured my lifejacket, tying two good knots.

I tried to ignore the maelstrom next to me. A clip from a film I had seen before I left home sprang into my mind: *Robinson Crusoe.* I could not have been further from a tropical paradise, but I remembered a scene in which Crusoe and Man Friday faced a fight with their dreaded enemies. The odds were against them, and they would most likely perish. Friday said:

'All men die. What matters is how you die.'

It was a corny line, I knew, but my panic subsided. At that

moment I made a simple promise, to myself. If I was going to die then I would die doing my best, trying my hardest and by helping others. I would not panic, or fall apart. I would not get into a life-raft without making sure that as many of the crew were as safe and as prepared as possible. Holding on to this resolution, I made my way back along the flooded deck.

.

14

15:55

Where were the officers of the *Sudur Havid* as we were abandoning? I thought someone would yell orders, co-ordinate a safe evacuation, act as a rock in our time of need. I thought each man would have his role to play: his radio call to make, his muster station to ready, his rescue bag with flares and radio to prepare. I was wrong.

If there was an order to abandon ship, no one heard it. The siren sequence reserved for emergencies went unused. If anyone was still below deck, they could be left behind. Bubbles watched us launch the rafts but was now lost in himself, staring out of the wheelhouse windows again. Boetie had disappeared from the bridge and was out of sight. Joaquim and Carlos, having helped to launch the life-rafts, had raced to the stern of the boat. Klaus and Glen, two of the highest-paid people on the boat, had merged into the crowd on deck, waiting rather than taking control. And where was Bjorgvin?

The three rafts were now all tethered near the stern, their bobbing orange canopies luminous against the dark clouds and grey sea. In just over an hour, the light would start to fade. Within two hours, it would be pitch-black. If rescue was coming, it needed to be quick. Standing on the deck between the rope crates and the funnel, I checked the crew around me; it was better to stay busy and not to think about it. Some were still unable to fasten their lifejackets and without the cords correctly tied they were useless. Trevor had his lifejacket properly secured, so I used him as an example. 'Like this, Kanime, over the head, straps round the back and tie!'

I tried to offer words of encouragement amid the confusion.

'Everything will be fine,' I said, as much to myself as to anyone else.

Charlie Baron joined me. He told me that, in the case of an abandon-ship, we should remove our boots. As well as hindering our swimming, they might have hooks in the soles that would rip the rubber rafts. I wasn't so sure. I didn't expect to swim far, and we would need as much insulation as possible, but I didn't argue and pulled them off. My feet shifted inside their layers of already soaked socks. The cold metal deck sucked away their heat. I made my way down the line of crew, checking that more lifejackets were on and that boots were off.

Eugene and Brian leant back against the guardrail and held up their feet so that I could pull the boots free. They could hardly bend over in their constricting lifejackets. Big Danie's boots were sealed so tightly over his ankles that the zips were jammed.

'Just keep them on, Danie, you'll be fine.'

I got to Alfius, the greaser and 'qualified second engineer'. He clutched a brown leather satchel to his chest. The rafts would be crowded enough without personal possessions. I was about to tell him to get rid of it, when I noticed it was tied to his lifejacket, through the straps. His eyes were wide, and he stuttered into his beard. The big man looked terrified. It was too small a matter to worry about, so I skipped on to the next person.

Mark was holding one of the large, rigid life-rings, sensibly not wanting to leave it on the boat.

'I'm taking it to the raft,' he said coolly.

'Just throw it in the water,' I replied, thinking it would get in the way. 'Maybe someone will need it there.' I watched as he threw it overboard, and the wind dragged it away.

A few deckhands had moved to the stern with the rafts, but most of the crew were now lined up next to me and waiting for instructions. I could see no reason to wait any longer. With no one else giving orders, I began shepherding them towards the rafts.

'Get to the stern of the ship! Your best chance to board is there.'

The ship was listing 45° to starboard now, and the extreme slope was making it harder to stand upright. Morné slid down the slippery deck into the alleyway. He jumped when he grabbed the handrail.

'Shit, I just got an electric shock off that!'

In my lifesaving training at secondary school, I was taught to yell to casualties 'Don't panic, stay calm!' At the time I had thought, 'Who would want to hear that? I bet you don't do that in real life.'

Now, as our lives were most in jeopardy, I fell back on what I had been trained to do. The queue of bodies slowly started to move past me, and I stood and shouted until my throat was hoarse.

'Keep calm, everything will be fine!'

It seemed to be working: no one was screaming or panicking. No one was waving knives around.

Looking back over the jumble of rope in the crates, I could see two of the rafts tucked in close to the stern, ready for boarding. A third raft was out on the end of its tether, fifteen metres or more clear of the boat. Its orange canopy looked brighter and newer than the others, and it was floating high in the water. Joaquim and Carlos were crouched inside its entrance. A thought flitted through my mind. Of all the rafts, my best chance of survival would be to stay with them. They were the most experienced fishermen aboard; they would know what to do. My mind was set. When it was my time to board, I would depart on their raft.

A bottleneck had developed and the alleyway was full of people. I walked across the coiled rope in the boxes to see what was causing the delay.

'Come on, guys, go, go, go!' I yelled.

The small deck, where we normally stood to shoot the line into the water, was crowded with men waiting to disembark, but no one was moving. Melvin straddled the safety rail at the starboard side, waiting for a raft to come closer. Big Danie blockaded the centre, trying to balance as the ship juddered. Eugene was clinging to the outside of the rail at the highest port side. The wind-chopped waves were tossing the rubber rafts around on their tethers. The twenty-man raft was just behind the *Sudur Havid*, and the twelve-man raft was just off to starboard. One moment we were in touching distance, the next they dropped down four metres in the swell. The doors in their orange canvas canopies were wide open and beckoning; the promise of sanctuary. The first few to board had managed to climb or jump across, but as the rafts grew heavier it was getting harder to keep them alongside. Now, those trying to abandon had to jump and it was a choice between a dangerous landing into the raft, or an ice-cold submersion in the water. Eugene was swaying, ready to jump but holding back, his eyes wide with fear.

'What's wrong, man?' I asked.

'The propeller, it's still turning!'

Just below him, under the hull, he could see its metal blades glinting in the swell. The propeller was almost two metres across, slowly churning the water. The boat was still in gear, slow ahead.

'Just jump, man, just jump!'

Eugene swayed back, readied himself and then launched his body into the air. Legs mid-stride, arms crossed over his chest, he disappeared under the water in a cloud of bubbles. He resurfaced, spluttering and gasping for air, before striking out for the larger raft.

Stephan climbed over the safety rail at the starboard edge of the stern, where it was closer to the water. Many of the Ovambo men were now in the rough water below us – some trying to swim, others clinging to one another, pushing each other under the surface in their panic and shock.

'My God, of course, they can't swim,' said Stephan. From our conversations in the factory, we knew this to be the case with most of the Ovambo and Cape Coloureds on board. Even in Stephan's home town, many of the fishermen had never learnt.

Hannes turned to him. 'Cousin, now it's every man for himself.'

There was no time to choose which raft to board. The smaller one was closer, anyway. He aimed to land as near as possible to the raft door, fearful that the height of the jump would push him underwater, like Eugene. With his lifejacket hooked over his right arm – he had not had time to put it on – he leapt out. His tall body fell through the air, his eyes closed.

When his body hit the water, his left arm caught the rubber tube rim of the raft, stopping him abruptly. The searing pain of the cold water against his legs and body tore into him, and he fought not to gulp in saltwater as his lungs cried out to inhale. Once he had caught his breath, he pulled himself up on to the edge of the raft and slumped inside.

The jam was resolved, the exodus from the *Sudur Havid* had resumed, and I looked up to check on the whereabouts of my favoured raft. I couldn't believe what I saw. Joaquim and Carlos had cut the painter and were drifting away on their own. They even waved. While we were faced with life-rafts carrying full loads, they had commandeered a life-raft fit for twelve.

Bastards.

Disgusted, I turned away.

Sven was also at the stern, having walked along the side of the hull. It was easier than trying to stagger along the deck. He could see barnacles, slime, rust and antifouling paint, all usually hidden below the waterline. Brian and Grant Forbes were next to him, holding on to each other.

'What's going to happen, Daddy?' Grant asked, 'What's going to happen now?'

Any father would try to allay his child's fear, however big that child had grown. But what was Brian to say? How could he relieve his only son's terror, when they both faced such desperate circumstances?

Sven looked down from the stern. There were more men in the water now: some swimming, some flailing and some trying to grab on to others. Sven clocked the nearest life-raft, gathered himself, and jumped. He landed in the water, next to Grant. The water penetrated every part of his freezer suit and clothing in an instant. It felt like needles hitting his skin. Knowing he had no lifejacket, he forced himself to swim as the nearest raft was only a few metres away. The propeller was behind him now, slowly churning but thankfully not pulling him in. Reaching the raft, he flung his arms up and over the tubes at the entrance. Charlie grabbed him, and helped him out of the water into the raft. Stephan, Grunter and Gideon were already there, as was Alfius. The life-raft was already a foot deep in water and no one was coming in dry. As each man had entered, the side of the raft had dipped, scooping in water and allowing the waves to crash in.

Someone passed Mark a small biltong knife and he used it to cut the painter holding them to the *Sudur Havid*. They began to drift away. Trying to move faster to get clear of the boat before it rolled on to them, they paddled, scooping water with their hands.

From his position next to the door in the canopy, Sven could see the *Sudur Havid* hanging in the waves, tilted at an unreal angle but still afloat. Grant Forbes was up to his neck in the water outside the raft, holding on to the ropes and calling out, but it was chaos inside. The raft was crowded, a jumble of recently arrived bodies.

'Hang on, Grant, we'll get to you now!' called Sven. When he turned back, Grant was gone.

Stephan sat, paralysed with the shock of the cold, at the edge of the raft. His body had seized up, and wouldn't respond. He watched Grant drift away from the raft. He was just a few metres off, but there was no way to reach him. Grant sank, arms up-stretched, hands still grasping for the raft, his bright-green oilskins disappearing down into the silver ocean.

16:00

A roaming albatross above, the soul of a dead sailor, would have seen the ship now prone in the water. Her engines were still running and smoke billowed from her exhausts, but her bow and starboard side were fully submerged, the rail slicing into the sea. Surf broke up her slanting decks and against her wheelhouse, sending clouds of spray whipping up and over her. Somehow, she had changed direction in the water. Maybe Boetie had steered a new course, in an attempt to shelter the hatches? Perhaps the boat had gradually been spun by the swells, or had been forced by one of the many huge waves? Whether swell or rudder, the *Sudur Havid* was now facing downwind.

I knew that I should be boarding a raft now, but I was concerned that people might still be below deck; I couldn't live with myself if we left someone behind. Above me, hanging on the portside guardrail, were the anchors for the fishing line, each forty-five kilos of rusty, crudely shaped iron. The boat lurched to starboard, and one of the anchors dislodged from its perch. It fell towards me, sliding along the tilting deck and hitting my shin before landing against the wall. My leg was pinned in the gap between the shaft and the metal funnel. We had enough to battle against without a broken leg. It was a lucky near-miss.

I climbed back up to the relative safety of the rope crates, and held on to the stern gantry. It was strange to look at the boat from this new viewpoint, tilted so far as it was from equilibrium. The deck was now eerily empty of crew. I heard a noise to my left. It was Bjorgvin, staggering out on deck. Bubbles had woken him from his sleep just minutes before.

'Bjorgvin!' Bubbles had called. 'Come at once!'

No one else had thought to rouse him. Accustomed to the rough ocean conditions and the noise of the working boat, he had slept through all the yelling and clattering feet as the pumps failed, and the preparations for abandonment, not to mention the weird motions of the boat as she took on water.

In the moments it took to dress, the boat fell to its starboard side, and Bjorgvin realized something was gravely wrong. He grabbed his orange deck-suit, similar to mine, from the hook on the back of the door and managed to get it half on. He emerged from his cabin to find the vessel almost completely devoid of people, and so low in the water that the starboard guardrail was disappearing under the waves.

'Matt, Matt, what is happening?'

His hair, usually neatly combed, was wild. He was clearly shaken by the state of the boat. I handed him a lifejacket and tried to be brief. There wasn't time for a long conversation.

'We've taken water into the factory deck, we're going down, everybody's abandoning ship.'

I climbed back up on to the portside guardrail of the ship, stepping along the edge of the rope crates as I picked my way towards the stern. At times, I was walking on the side of the hull, impossible but for the extreme tilt. I stood on the stern gantry and turned for one last look. So this was what a doomed ship looked like.

Bjorgvin was down by the starboard guardrail, bent over and struggling with something. A bag? Possessions? What could he be doing?

'Bjorgvin, come on, man, come on!' I yelled. 'We have got to get off the boat!'

'No, no, no . . .' but his voice was carried away by the wind. I turned and climbed back. His words became understandable.

'I'm trying to save Bubbles.'

Hidden from my view, down behind the rope crates, Bubbles had collapsed on the deck awash in freezing seawater. He was now leant on the starboard rail, being pummelled by the waves. Bjorgvin scrambled down to push him up, but Bubbles was too weak to climb. Using a rope, Bjorgvin heaved Bubbles out of the water and into the dry alleyway. Bubbles leant on my shoulder as he shuffled towards the rafts, and Bjorgvin pulled his suit up and zipped it shut. He then handed Bubbles his own lifejacket. Wearing only a jumper and jogging bottoms, Bubbles would not stand a chance in the sea without it.

I helped Bubbles knot the straps of the lifejacket as Bjorgvin climbed over the guardrail at the stern, and crouched down. Only one raft was tied to the boat, and he lowered himself as far as he could. If at all possible, he wanted to avoid landing in the water. At sixty years of age, he was not sure he would have the strength to swim and haul himself into the raft. When it was almost underneath him, Bjorgvin let go and dropped, slithering down the raft's canopy and in through the door.

With my arms under his shoulders, Bubbles lay on top of the guardrail and swung his legs over. I eased him down to lie awkwardly between my feet and the rail, clutching the thick wool of his jumper to steady him. His face was ash-grey. Balanced on the ledge at the very stern of his boat, he lay passively as we waited for the raft to come close enough.

Below us, Morné knelt at the edge of the raft. A knife was unsheathed in his hand, ready to cut the painter to free the raft as soon as we were aboard.

'Morné, watch your knife, you'll cut the Skipper!' I yelled. He put his knife away. Bubbles was twice my weight so there was no way I could lift him into the raft, but I couldn't miss and drop him into the water either.

Christ, the raft seemed to be dropping a long way from the boat. I looked down at Bubbles, and caught his eye. Even in this fleeting instant, it was obvious that something was wrong. Gone was the robust, assertive Bubbles. Instead, he looked like a ghost.

The swell lifted the raft back up towards us. Morné and Hannes knelt ready at the entrance, with their arms outstretched. The raft was as close as it would be. I released my grip, and let Bubbles tumble the last few feet into the embrace of his crew.

I looked along the deck one last time, just to check. No one was left on the boat but me. The *Sudur Havid* deserved a better end than this. It was clear that the ship was doomed, and that we were right to be boarding the rafts. Joaquim and Carlos's raft had already drifted thirty metres or more from the boat, and was now well out of reach. I could see Joaquim leaning out of the raft, his hands under the shoulders of someone in the water. Was it Albert? A huge swell moved through, and they were hidden from sight. A second raft was closer to the *Sudur Havid*, dropping and rising by the rusted white gantry slightly forward of me, but it would be awkward to reach.

The third and final raft, the largest of the three, was floating under me at the stern. There would be no need to swim. I held the rail with one hand behind me, and shifted my stance so that I was poised to jump. I waited for the raft to rise up on the next swell, until it was just a few metres below. The door was wide open. Letting go of the guardrail I leapt, like a kid in a ball pool, into the raft below me. Landing on my backside in the midst of a tangle of bodies, I was almost dry. My body was flooded with adrenaline. I wasn't scared, I was exhilarated. Whatever was going to happen, at least we were off the sinking ship. I was the last man off.

THREE

ADRIFT

16

16:04

Hannes, Bubbles, Simon, Brian, Jerimia, Morné, Bjorgvin, Haimbodi, Boetie, Big Danie, Eugene, Kenny, Kanime, Trevor, David and me. The weak light of winter illuminated the life-raft through its canopy, but it was so crowded and chaotic that it was difficult to see the faces crowded inside.

I had heard tales of mariners being dragged underwater by sinking vessels. But I had also heard that a crew should stay with their boat as long as possible, that the best chance of rescue was with the ship, the biggest search target. If we stayed tethered, we risked entanglement with the wreckage. Cut free, we could drift away from potential salvation. As we weighed up these options, the wind and the waves hurled us back against the *Sudur Havid*, smashing us against the steel hull. This was enough to make up our minds. We had to get away.

Having persuaded Morné to stow his knife, now we couldn't find it, or any other knife, for that matter. Everyone on board searched frantically through their pockets and clothes. The waves heaved us back towards the boat. I found myself kneeling at the canopy doorway, and cowered away from the massive hull as it loomed over us.

The *Sudur Havid*'s half-flooded factory deck pulled the bow under first. She pivoted, and the dark-blue stern reared into the air. Blown back under the boat as it hung above us, we rose and fell metres at a time amid the house-sized swells; at every moment our tiny raft was threatened with destruction. Before I could brace myself a devastating swell picked up the raft and sent us hurtling towards the ship. My head banged hard against the hull, dragging across the rough red paintwork of the underside as we continued to ride the ocean's current. The pitted metal came down against my back; the force was overwhelming. It felt as though my body would pop. Had I fought so hard to save the boat, just to be crushed by her? In desperation I punched and slapped at the thick iron plate, cursing her for letting us down.

Next to me, Hannes and Boetie were locked in their own futile battle. Like ants pushing back against the boot that squashed them, they strained to keep us away from the *Sudur Havid*. With fuel and catch she now weighed over 700 tonnes. There was nothing we could do to stop her.

Relenting momentarily, we rolled away just enough to pop out from underneath her. The swells took us in the right direction away from the hull – five metres of freedom – only for the wind and the painter to reel us back. Crouched in the entrance of the raft, I pitied the others inside who were blind to the same confusing onslaught and battering; unsure when to push or to brace, or which way to escape.

It felt as if the boat were out to kill us. The underside of the stern tried to crush us, and the once-protective railings were now sharp edges to catch and tear the rubber tubes. We continued to be driven along the starboard side of the hull by the irresistible double act of the wind and the waves but now the ship began to roll further over towards us. The huge engine chimney casing bore down. Exhaust pipes belching hot fumes loomed just metres above our heads. With the engines still running, the pipes would be hot enough to melt our rubber raft. I watched in horror as we were raised by a swell, and the scorching pipes came closer and closer to our fragile sanctuary. Surely they would burn us?

While some waves seemed to carry us towards imminent death,

others seemed to save us. We were swept clear of the ship, only to be snapped back again by the painter or another swell. The collision of inflatable raft against hull threw Hannes back on to the boat. One minute he was with us, the next he was left clinging to the side of the rope crates, his arms wrapped around the rails.

'What are you doing?' I yelled. 'Get back on the raft!'

While Hannes was clinging to the boat, the raft rebounded to the end of the rope tether. We were desperate to get away before the *Sudur Havid* sank but needed him back before we could escape. A well-timed wave brought us within jumping distance and Hannes leapt safely back in the raft.

Morné had found a safety cutter, a small plastic item the size of a credit card, attached to the inside of the raft. He passed the serrated blade to Big Danie, who cut the painter. We pushed to get free, but the wind blew us against the hull. A quick search of the raft found nothing that resembled paddles, so we tried to propel the twenty-man raft against the wind with our hands. This had no effect, but after one more bounce against the boat we seemed to move away.

Just when we thought we were clear, the boat shifted and the stern gantry came slamming down. This arch of heavy steel had once supported the trawl cables, but now the girders were slicing down on to the raft's roof, folding the raft in two and forcing us underwater. The gantry caught my head: an irresistible force bearing down on me through the canvas canopy. The flat steel pressed against my skull so hard I wanted to cry out, but I was being smothered. Cold water rushed past my cheek. The raft flooded instantly as its rim was submerged. Frigid grey seawater plunged in, swirling around us. To my right, Morné felt someone push his head underwater at the last second, narrowly avoiding the full brunt of the crushing gantry. Fighting for breath, it felt as though he was metres below the surface.

And then we were free. The boat shifted in the water and the gantry relinquished its hold. We were less buoyant now but still afloat and the wind and waves carried us slowly away. Our collision with the gantry had flooded the raft with thousands of litres of freezing seawater. Only the top tube of the raft now sat clear of the ocean's surface; the other two that formed the walls were submerged. The floor bowed down away from us, sagging under the weight of the flooding. This made standing difficult and we were up to our waists and chests in $-1°C$ seawater. But, thank God, we were leaving the boat behind.

The *Sudur Havid* was our one reference point in the storm. There was no land to gauge our movements by, the sea and sky gave no clue as to our whereabouts; we had no idea in which direction safety lay. Without paddles, we could not dictate our movement either. For a few minutes we drifted within sight of the *Sudur Havid* as her list grew worse and her bow sank from view. The engine was still running, its low steady rumble clearly audible against the noise of the sea.

It wasn't silence that was left when the engine finally stopped, but it felt like it. The wind continued howling and the waves were still crashing, but the thrum of the engine and the burbling of the exhaust, which had been our near-constant percussion for the last two months, just stopped.

I didn't see her sink; I missed her final moments. I don't think I could have borne seeing our life support system disappear from in front of us.

Morné watched her go. The bow sank down first, the wheelhouse still visible. She then seemed to come back to level again – one final fight – but then the bow lifted from the water and she descended silently stern first. Was it the sudden flooding of the engine room that caused the engines to cease? Was that the final straw? We would never know. There was nothing around us now but the other two rafts, the waves and the wind. Barely any debris, even.

★

A few minutes later, I discovered Hannes was holding a man, supporting him in the water next to the raft. It was Peinge. Where had he come from? I thought we were all in the rafts?

'Quick, Hannes, let's get him in'

'No, no, you know we can't!'

The raft was already full of people and seawater.

'No, let's get him in!'

Grabbing fistfuls of oilskins, we pulled Peinge up as far as we could but his legs were catching on ropes in the water. Hannes leant out of the raft and reached into the water to free his legs. Once he was released, I hauled Peinge up and together we fell into the water inside the life-raft.

Peinge wasn't even struggling. He just lay there in the water, sprawled on top of me, lifeless. His ebony eyes were half closed, and his dark face and beard were framed by the candid colours of his lifejacket and bobble hat. Immersion in such cold water had sent his body into shock and it was shutting down.

I hoisted his head and shoulders above the water and shook him.

'Breathe! Fight!'

As if you could command someone to live. These were out-of-place orders from an out-of-depth officer. But suddenly he gasped. His eyes opened. Hannes freed the last of the rope from his legs, and we were able to roll him over. He lay enfolded by his lifejacket, the water inside the raft supporting him now. At least he was no longer alone.

The ties that held the flaps of the doors open were impossibly tight. Brian and I forced our fingertips into the canvas knots, to try and release them. With our hands embittered by the cold it took us a several minutes just to loosen them. Once dropped, the flaps offered some protection from the wind and we could turn our attention to the water inside. I knew from my training as a SCUBA diver that water conducts heat away from the body twenty-five times faster than air. Our chances of survival had to be better if we could stay clear of the water so I checked the raft for supplies again. We were still missing paddles and bailers.

'Danie, give me your boot!' We would have to improvise.

The water and his wet socks meant that Danie could no longer pull it off himself, so he raised his leg and I tugged the wellington from his foot. Once removed, I raised it from the water like a trophy.

'Bloody hell! You could bail the *Titanic* with that!' We burst out laughing, the absurd comedy a welcome break from reality.

I checked again for supplies. For some reason, we had an empty Nescafé Gold jar in our raft, an item not normally listed in essential survival manuals. Still, it could be used. All counted, we had five wellington boots and a Nescafé jar to bail the raft.

As I crouched at the opening with Morné and Brian, we started to bail. Hannes and Big Danie worked at the opening on the opposite side of the raft. With my cold hands working as fast as they could, my thoughts turned to Bubbles. He had not looked well as I manhandled him into the raft and I was starting to suspect that he had suffered a heart attack. I couldn't see him through the canopy opening and imagined him slipping below the water inside. Kenny appeared next to me, his gold tooth glinting. Kenny was usually one of the most cheerful deckhands aboard, but now he seemed horror-struck. His eyes darted around the featureless sea as he fought to get his bearings. He needed a distraction.

'Kenny, you go back inside, I want an answer. You tell me if Bubbles is OK? If he is above the water?'

Kenny stooped back into the raft. He emerged a minute later.

'Yes, Matt, Bubbles is here. He is OK.'

The life-raft was a metre deep in water. At three metres in diameter, this meant that several thousand litres of seawater swilled inside. The boots were useless as bailers; their thin rubber collapsed the moment it hit the water. Our icy fingers were also now too stiff to hold them open. I realized that we were only removing a litre of water, at the most, over the side with each slow scoop.

At first we bailed through both hatches on the raft, but the waves breaking over us and bursting through the windward side were undoing all of our hard work. Hannes and Big Danie held the windward hatch closed, and Morné and I bailed through the leeward opening instead. But when the raft rotated this soon suffered the same problem and the water poured back in. With the doors held closed, I tried bailing through a gap between the tubes and the canopy, but the amount I could discharge was piteous.

Keeping the doors open to bail also meant losing any heat that we had built up inside the raft. We would have to rely on our bodies now to warm the water, and for rescue to arrive before our bodies gave out. Perhaps the gantry hadn't just flooded the vessel? With such heavy metalwork on the move, it may well have ripped the floor. Whether the raft was holed or not was impossible to see. In the dying sub-Antarctic winter light, the waist-deep water was black.

Brian had last seen his only son, Grant, in the water heading towards another raft. He did not know what Sven and Stephan had witnessed, and was still concerned for Grant's safety. Brian knew that he couldn't swim – he had never learnt himself – but he had to hope that his son was safe.

We busied ourselves checking the raft for more supplies. Morné opened the bag that Bubbles had been packing on the bridge and looked inside. It contained our passports, Joaquim's video camera and a bottle of KWV brandy. What a disappointment. Where were the EPIRBs, the handheld VHF radio and the flares?

Two bags had been seen floating outside. Hannes retrieved them, but the list of contents on the packs was illegible in the dim light. With no knives to hand, we tore the packs open with our teeth, only to find food sachets and water – neither of which we saw ourselves as needing.

'Throw them away, get rid of the weight!' said Hannes.

'No, no! Don't throw the food away, we might need it!' replied Boetie.

Perhaps they had been washed or torn away in our battering as we departed, but if there had been any other supplies or equipment in the raft, we couldn't find them now. We had no way to communicate with the outside world, and no way to attract the attention of potential rescuers. There were no paddles or bailers and, crucially, no sea anchor. The latter was a big loss. Like an underwater parachute, it would have dragged below us through the water to stabilize the raft and stop us from spinning around. Instead, we were at the mercy of the wind that could blow us far away from the potential search area. The pull of the anchor would also have slowed us down and kept us facing in one direction, which would have allowed us to bail and keep watch through the protected leeward hatch. It would have made us ride the swells more comfortably too. Bjorgvin had swallowed seawater as we were pushed under by the gantry, and the relentless circling and rise and fall of the raft was now causing him to cough and be sick.

Eugene was determined to have one last cigarette and had managed to keep a packet dry in a polythene bag inside his clothing. He passed one to Big Danie and Morné, too, and they tried to light them.

Again and again, the lighter refused to spark up, even when Eugene used his old trick of drying the wheel on the brim of his woolly hat. Morné waited with the cigarette in his lips but a wave hit the raft and swept through. The cigarette was washed from his mouth instantly, the packet lost to the ocean.

We needed to fasten the doors, to seal out the weather. Until now we had been relying on an elastic hem on the door, but this was not strong enough to hold against a wave or a strong gust. Inside the doors, Morné and I found inch-wide Velcro straps. Once threaded through an eyelet, these could be attached to a corresponding patch on the rubber tube. It was not an easy task and, as our fingers chilled, it became more and more awkward.

Infuriatingly, each time I succeeded in fastening the strap, a large wave swept through and crashed against the canopy, ripping open the doors and soaking us. My bare hands stiffened. I knelt in the water, holding the flap of the life-raft down with my teeth while I threaded the Velcro strap through the eyelet with my two numb hands. Finally, after I strapped the last Velcro down, I leant back to admire my handiwork once more. Seconds later the hatch ripped open again.

We abandoned our attempts to bail and retreated to find our own spaces within the raft, jostling for positions at the edge, away from the deepest water in the centre. I managed to squeeze myself into a gap at the back of the raft and hooked my arm over the rope that ran around the inner edge of the tube. Resting like this, I kept my feet moving to prevent me from slipping back into the centre of the raft. Like walking on a treadmill, my socks slipped on the slope of the bowed floor, and I trudged ceaselessly. I was running a marathon, without getting anywhere.

Boetie suddenly stood up next to me and tore open the door.

'Boetie, get inside!' I protested.

Swaying at full height, and gripped with panic and claustrophobia, Boetie looked crazed as he scanned the ocean.

'We must open the hatches!' he cried. 'We have to see the other life-rafts.'

17

16:10

Stephan was still reeling with shock from the sight of Grant sinking below the waves. He looked at the faces around his own crowded raft: Klaus, Gideon, Grunter, Glen, Charlie, Efeinge, Matheus, Alfius, Sven, Mark, Vendadu, Walu Walu and Little Danie. Hannes was not inside. He prayed that his cousin had made it to another raft but hadn't seen him since the abandon-ship and feared he was adrift in the water. The light in the raft was tinted orange by the canopy, as in a tent. Charlie Baron's voice rang out over the clamour of the storm, and interrupted his thoughts.

'We must form a circle. Backs against the tubes, legs pointing towards the centre. Let's brace the raft and keep it stable.'

Only two and a half metres in diameter, the raft was at risk of capsizing if everyone was thrown to one side. Stephan shuffled around. Thankfully, the paralysis from his immersion in cold water had faded. Like slices of cake, fourteen men sat shoulder to shoulder around the perimeter of the life-raft built for twelve. Their lifejackets, so bulky on their chests and around their necks, made them feel even more cramped. Charlie tied a short length of rope to a lifejacket, ready to throw it to the voices he had heard outside. Bitter-cold water washed over their thighs. In the centre of the raft, their feet disappeared under grey murk as the water sloshed around. Stephan's toes were numb but he tried to move them in his socks.

Across the raft, Walu Walu, the winch man, seemed to be more concerned with his mobile phone than with the actual threat they faced. During the abandon-ship he grabbed his prized possession from his cabin, and he held it now, wrapped in a plastic bag. Again and again, sat in the deep seawater, he pulled it out from the chest pocket of his navy-blue freezer suit to check that it was still dry. Alfius, meanwhile, clutched his leather briefcase tightly to his body.

Charlie found one of the raft's survival bags and tore it open. He handed Sven and Mark a small plastic bucket each to bail with before carefully rolling the bag shut. Sitting next to one another on the floor, Sven looked at Mark as they began scooping and tipping the water over their shoulders. Mark was dripping wet and shivering. At least the work would warm him up.

At first it felt as if they were hardly making a difference. The bailers were so small – the size of children's toys – and there was so much water in the raft. But together they developed a system. After closing the windward canopy door, Mark and Sven bailed through the leeward opening. If the raft rotated, they changed doors and Charlie took over bailing. Working this way for thirty minutes or so, Sven realized that they had reduced the flooding to just a few inches. Cold and exhausted, they finally took a break.

Charlie opened the door wide to check on the other rafts. Bracing himself against Stephan's shoulder, he stood up to scan around. The light was fading. From such a low vantage point in the constantly shifting seascape, it was difficult to see very far. He waited for the swells to lift them up. A raft appeared, just fifty metres away, downwind. It was low in the water, and Charlie could see Hannes at the doorway, beckoning. As it rode the swells, Charlie saw that the raft was bending and forming to the shape of the sea. The canopy was bowed in on the windward side, beaten in by the force of the wind and the waves.

He scanned around again, this time looking farther out, still searching for the third raft. He waited for the swells to shift around and reveal a speck of bright colour against the pale sea, but nothing appeared.

Charlie knew it would be better to bring the two rafts together before nightfall. He rooted around in the bag of supplies, and handed Sven and Mark two small paddles from the supplies bag. 'Start rowing, guys!'

'How the hell are we supposed to row with wooden spoons?' Mark snorted in disgust.

Knelt at the doorway, the two deckhands dug at the water. The raft was heavy with the weight of fourteen men, but if they opened the other doorway, so that more of the crew could start paddling, it would let in more waves. One moment, it felt like they were making progress, but then the sea shifted and the other raft seemed to jump further away. The gap seemed to drop from fifty to thirty metres, and then leapt back up again. After five minutes of paddling, the rafts looked further apart. Mark and Sven stopped. Keeping the canopy open was stripping away any heat they had left and it would take too long to bring the two vessels together. They had to think of their own raft. Charlie closed the flaps.

Although they were now more sheltered and together as a group, Sven and the crew felt more vulnerable and isolated. Instead of fighting to bail, or paddling to bring the rafts together, they were sat waiting in silence, listening to the thunderous noise outside. The wind screamed and tore at the canopy, flailing the canvas. When the spray lashed against the fabric, it sounded as if someone was pelting them with handfuls of gravel.

Every few minutes Sven heard the roar of cascading water bearing down on them, getting closer and closer. He couldn't see anything but felt the raft begin to lift, and braced himself for the hit. If the swell began to break with the raft at its crest, they would surely be sent somersaulting.

When it came, the force of the water colliding with the raft buckled their legs, collapsing their neatly braced circle. The swells were like unstoppable ocean liners but it was the chops blown by the wind that were steeper and that were breaking over the raft. After the chop passed through, those thrown into the centre scrambled to get back to a stable position before the next wave came rolling in. The metal hull of the boat had offered such protection from the elements compared to their fragile rubber and canvas raft. Now there was no escape from the noise and the power of the ocean.

Stephan felt a long way from his family in Cape Town. His little sister was only ten years old, and it didn't seem fair that he wouldn't see her again. She was so small and he could almost feel her in his arms, giving him a hug goodbye. Snapshots of his life flashed before him and dissolved, from catching a fish with his dad when he was a boy, to splitting with his fiancée just before he had left on the *Sudur Havid*.

Gideon called out across the raft. 'I'm hungry, is there any food?'

Charlie had found some ration packs in the bag and gave them some of the biscuits. It was hard to believe that someone was thinking of their stomach at a time like this, but Gideon was still only a teenager. Charlie had lost track of his older brother, Albert, as they abandoned the *Sudur Havid*. He was not in the raft and Charlie just had to hope that he was safe. God help anyone who was still in the water.

Charlie asked Sven to assemble what looked like a radio transmitter. He couldn't get his own hands to work due to the cold and held them up to Sven as evidence – his stiff fingers were useless. Sven examined the device. He had seen EPIRBs back on the boat, but this one looked different – the fibreglass antenna fitted together like a fishing rod and then slotted into the metal body. After a few minutes he thought he understood what he needed to do, but he couldn't get his hands to perform the simple task, as many times as he tried. Cupping his hands to his mouth he breathed on them, trying to infuse them with some warmth, but they were chilled to the bone. His concentration started to drift and he thought about his family back at home in the Strand, near Cape Town. It would be getting dark and his dad would be sitting at the old wooden table, a drink in his hand. Maybe his brother would be lighting the braai outside. Tiredness was beginning to get the better of Sven; he just wanted to close his eyes.

Charlie whacked him on the forehead with one of the little paddles from the survival bag.

'Sven, wake up, you can't sleep! Keep busy with something, don't just sit there and do nothing!'

But with his hands so deadened he could do little to occupy himself. Eventually, Sven opened the door and dumped the EPIRB antenna outside. He might not be able to fit it together, but he reasoned that at least if it floated in the sea, it might emit a signal. Although his hands were too cold to be of any use, he felt the rest of his body beginning to warm up. It was a bizarre sensation, but he reasoned that his circulation was finally starting to fight the cold.

The chops roared in, one after the other, and Stephan gripped on to the rope to anchor himself. They seemed to have been in the raft for hours. Charlie gave the occasional orders, 'keep busy', 'don't sleep' or 'brace'. From time to time, he opened the door to peek into the night, scanning for other rafts or for some sign of a rescue.

The daylight outside had faded, and unbroken cloud cover blocked any further light from the moon and the stars. The strobe on the peak of the roof, flashing its way through the night, shone through the canopy. The raft, meanwhile, compressed from side to side with each passing wave. Each time the men braced themselves and then pushed the walls of the raft back to retain its shape, and to stop the vessel from capsizing. Thinking logically, Stephan could not see how they could survive. He had seen only one other boat on the grounds in two months at sea, and that had been many weeks ago.

Across the raft, Klaus mumbled to himself. Grunter was quietly praying aloud, while his son Gideon lay on the floor in the shallow water next to him. Gideon seemed to be too weak to sit up, and looked like he was close to death, but Grunter didn't appear to be too worried. Stephan thought he looked curiously peaceful for a man whose son was busy dying.

Stephan looked at Sven, who was still clutching the body of the EPIRB. He was shivering so violently that Stephan could see his shoulders shaking, but his head was nodding as he drifted towards sleep.

'Sven, wake up!'

As far as Stephan was concerned, Sven was the only man aboard capable of putting the EPIRB together, but he was too cold to reply properly. He slapped Sven hard across the face.

'You can't go to sleep here, you'll die here.'

18

17:00

'Matt, where is the boat?'

Voices in the raft sought answers from someone who might know. Bubbles lay quiet, Boetie was incoherent and Bjorgvin was still being sick after swallowing too much seawater. At least there was no smell of vomit – the sea saw to that.

'Matt, is there a boat coming to save us?'

'I don't know.'

I couldn't bring myself to give a full answer. Although I had heard the voice on the radio as we escaped, I wasn't even sure if they had received our position. I knew that the *Northern Pride* was a hundred miles away, which would take more than ten hours of steaming: too far. There were only supposed to be ten other boats around South Georgia, and I hadn't seen any on radar since we refuelled. There was no one close to us.

We were 200 miles from King Edward Point, but the Royal Engineers on the island had only a few small shore boats. The nearest helicopter was on Falkland, 700 miles west, which would be beyond its range.

Morné turned to David. He had been shipwrecked before, in the warm waters of Mauritius.

'When your boat sank before, how long did it take to get rescued?' Morné asked quietly.

'Not this long. Half an hour,' David replied.

Morné had hoped for some encouragement. Disappointed, he sank back into his thoughts.

For some, the shock of the cold and the stress began to affect their behaviour. Boetie had been groaning for some time, his distinctive nasal voice ringing out across the raft. I knew he had been hit hard by the gantry, and he must have been hurting, but there was no way to help him. His groaning grew quieter, and less frequent. Worried, I looked across to check on him. He was still standing with his shoulders hunched and his head leant against the canopy. Still standing meant still alive.

A new voice filled the void with its wailing. It was much higher in pitch than before and almost female in its tone. Kenny, normally so boisterous and macho in the factory, was crying out. The help-lessness and anguish in each utterance was unbearable. His cries grated against the survival instincts firing in my head; the polar opposite of my determination to stay alive. After minutes of lis-tening to his soul-destroying howls, which obscured everything but the beating of the waves, I snapped.

'Who's making those noises? Will you bloody well be quiet?'

Kenny fell silent. As brutal as it was to silence someone pleading for help, it worked. The mood in the raft seemed to improve, returning to expectant waiting.

Glimpsing out of the canopy door I spied the raft that had launched next to ours, now some distance away – fifty metres, per-haps more. The third raft with Carlos and Joaquim had disappeared from view as we boarded; no one could remember having seen it since. The light on the top of the other raft's roof blinked emphat-ically against the darkening sky. I looked up to the peak of our own raft. The plastic strobe light wasn't working. I checked inside but there were no clues to be had, and no connections to be made. This part of the raft had been hit hard by the gantry and might well have been damaged. I wondered how we could expect to be found in the darkness, and whether the raft could survive in its damaged state.

Before night finally descended, it seemed logical to attempt to bring the two rafts together – strength in numbers; two needles together in a haystack. Hannes and I yelled across to the other raft, signalling our intention, and we began paddling with our hands. Encouragingly, they responded. Mark and Sven knelt at their own canopy door, with what seemed to be small oars, and began propelling themselves forward. We got to within thirty metres but then they seemed to be pulled further away. We renewed our efforts.

After a few minutes, it was obvious that they were not enough. The gap was growing and we were at the mercy of the sea. We stopped, and so did they. I wondered if they had decided not to bridge the gap. Did they know how bad things had become in our raft? Did they think their own vessel would be in danger if they tried to help us? Admittedly, their own raft looked to be in better condition, was higher in the water and was lit. I wouldn't blame them if they had decided not to meet. Who would want to spend the night in a flooded raft, when tied closely to a dry one? If all of us tried to climb into theirs, it would be carnage. Maybe it was for the best that they couldn't reach us.

However, faced with the prospect of a night of drifting alone, and invisible to rescuers without a strobe light, my thoughts changed. If we couldn't get the two rafts together, could we swim to them?

Boetie, Hannes and I sat at the door to discuss our options. Boetie seemed to be *compos mentis* again. We looked at the gap between the rafts, which was fifty metres, but it seemed to be growing. The light was fading and this could be our last chance. All three of us could swim, but could we swim so far in these conditions, when our arms and legs were already so cold? I had heard of competent swimmers drowning close to shore in warmer and calmer waters, their bodies disabled by the cold and fatigue, but I was desperate to escape the raft.

'Look, I've got this suit that floats, and we've all got lifejackets . . .' I said.

'I don't have a lifejacket,' answered Boetie.

I stooped back inside the cover and found one floating free in the centre. Someone must have removed it. We continued our assessment. The surge of the waves made the other raft appear to move impossibly far away and then feasibly near. The swells were immense. Would we be able to make any progress swimming up a wave ten metres in height? Or would we just get crushed underwater by a breaking crest and battered around, trying to stay afloat? Would the wind blow us away? I couldn't bear to think of what might happen if we lost sight of the other raft.

There was no way we would make it, I decided, and ducked back inside the flooded raft. The others agreed, and we closed up the door as best as we could. There was nowhere safe that could be reached, and we had failed in our attempts to bail the raft. Someone would have to help us now; we were in no position to save ourselves. Resigned to wait, I waded through the centre, now over a metre deep in ice-cold water, passing Kenny on the way. He was lying on his side awkwardly in his lifejacket, staring blankly ahead. I found a spot at the edge of the raft, next to the pillar supporting the roof. I was able to squeeze between David and Big Danie, who were lying lower in the water, and twist my arm through the rope around the perimeter. The thin cord dug in, but it kept me stable.

I kept myself busy, checking that my suit was zipped up properly, and that my collar was pulled up as far as it would go. I tried to climb higher out of the water, but slipped on the rubber floor in my socks. Maybe this cycle of constant adjustment would keep me going and prolong my survival. The chill was spreading through my body.

Morné called out from the other side of the raft:

'Someone help me . . . with this cover.'

Reaching him meant wading through the waist-deep water, and negotiating a tangle of ropes, legs and lifejackets that people had discarded. Once again, I threaded the thin straps through the plastic eyelets to fasten the canopy down. I knew that my work would be undone in a few minutes, torn open by the wind. There had to be a better way to secure the straps but if we tied them, instead of relying on the Velcro, then we would be trapped inside. After helping Morné, I went back across the raft. There was no gap to rest in by the door, and no way to climb out of the water.

I pushed against David with my shoulder, trying to squeeze into a position around the perimeter of the raft. He shuffled across to make a little room for me, but there was still barely enough space to fit in. My lifejacket had shifted when we had abandoned, and the ties that had seemed so secure were now loose and tangling around my thighs. The cumbersome foam blocks were preventing me from finding a restful position. I tore it off over my head, and tossed it away. We were in a life-raft now, I reasoned. I shouldn't need it any more.

A thin rope ran around the inside edge of the raft like a handrail, tied at intervals to the inflatable tubes. I knew I needed to get as far out of the water as possible, to preserve body heat. With great difficulty, I managed to manoeuvre one leg over the rope so that now I was sitting astride it. Next to me, the inflatable pillar of the arch that held up the canopy offered some support. Forcing my hand around the back of the pillar against the seam of the canopy I clung to the column, like a frightened child hugging his father's leg.

I hoped I could stay like this for some time with my upper body out of the water. The cord cut into my right thigh. My leg, already numb from the cold, felt dead. How long, I wondered, could we survive? A night-time rescue seemed unlikely. Could we make it through until morning?

There was now a gentle orange glow in the raft emanating from the lights on the shoulders of the lifejackets. They lit up when in contact with the seawater, but had only become noticeable as darkness had fallen. With my head laid against the canopy, I closed my eyes and started to quietly sing.

> *Will your anchor hold in the storms of life,*
> *When the clouds unfold their wings of strife . . .*

My memory failed me so I launched into the chorus:

> *We have an anchor that keeps the soul*
> *Steadfast and sure while the billows roll.*

I learnt the song at Sunday school when I was ten years old. I used to gaze out through the church window at the rich green meadows and wooded hills of Somerset. Finally, years later and 8000 miles away from home, it couldn't be more appropriate.

On the other side of the raft, Morné felt a pain in his foot. Fumbling underwater with his numbed fingers, he touched something clamping around his toes. In the twilight, he couldn't see what was causing him such pain.

'Christ . . . Danie . . . there's something on my foot!'

Big Danie reached down into the water to help him, and struggled to lift Morné's leg from the water. Up with it came a body, its mouth clamped on to Morné's toes. Danie shrank back. It was one of his fellow pot-makers. He was dead.

In the darkness, it was impossible to work out who he was. When they managed to release him, he slumped into the water. With no lifejacket, he disappeared back under the surface. He was just a corpse now, and Morné wondered how much he was weighing the raft down.

'There's more than one,' Danie said. When he moved his stiff legs, other bodies thudded against them.

'We should throw them out,' suggested Morné.

They were so cold that they barely had the energy to speak, let alone lift a man and dump him overboard. The risk of opening the canopy, and the troubles of closing it again, was all too much. The bodies stayed where they were.

Another half an hour or so must have passed, although my watch was hidden by layers of clothing. Boetie's voice broke the silent waiting, snapping us out of our quiet thoughts.

'Hey, guys, you know, we must all get into the water, this life-raft is sinking.'

'Huh?'

'No, guys, guys, we must all get into the water, we must all hold hands, this life-raft is gonna sink.'

Boetie's reasoning was fatally flawed. We were in an inflatable rubber raft and, even though it was leaking, it was not about to sink.

'We'll be fine if we all hold hands. Let's make a circle in the water.'

So this was Boetie's survival plan? Our chances in the water were clear to me.

'No one leaves this fucking life-raft!' I yelled out. 'No one leaves this raft!'

I would have no more discussion.

The raft fell silent. The canopy was rubbing against my head, but next to my face a sleeve led to a hole in the canopy, presumably for ventilation or an antenna. Through it a cold draught blew across Big Danie and me. Each time I pulled the cord to shut the sleeve, it would blow open again. With no toggle on the cord to lock it closed, and with my fingers too frigid to tie a knot, it became one more repetitive task with which to occupy my thoughts. The wind blew the sleeve open; I pulled it closed. I was already trying to hold myself upright with one hand, and cinch the cord tight with the other. Danie tried too, but I was worried he would pull it so hard that the canopy would rip open.

After many attempts, I gave up closing the ventilation sleeve, and made myself as comfortable as possible. The pillar felt softer than before; the raft must have been leaking somewhere. Time passed, though I had no way to tell how much. How long had we been adrift?

'Hannes, Hannes, help me,' Boetie called, imploring his favourite crewman. 'Somebody help me, please . . .'

You stupid fool, I thought. *You're going to die if you don't help yourself. You need to fight! Why are you yelling for your crew to help you?* We were all fighting for our own survival.

Morné and I were still trying to fasten down the door of the raft but the wind kept blowing it open. Each time the raft was invaded by a blast of wind and saltwater, the precious warmth was stripped away. We were still intent on fixing the door, but our fingers were so stiff now that it was almost impossible. I went back to my position straddling the rope by the pillar. Morné wrapped the fabric of the door around his knuckles, and rammed his hand down outside the tube. He held it shut; his hand versus the sub-Antarctic storm outside.

Bubbles lay in the water in the centre of the raft. His head was supported by the collar of his lifejacket, and his hands were tucked into his barrel chest. He had survived all this time in only a chunky-knit jumper and tracksuit bottoms. They could offer no protection against the freezing water, the biting wind and the hypothermia, let alone the heart attack that he might have suffered. Bjorgvin and I had seen him collapsed on the deck. Even then his skin had looked pale and grey. But there was nothing we could do to help him now. This was the man who had sung 'Flower of Scotland' over the radio to the Harbour Master on South Georgia each week, as we reported our catches. He had a wife and two teenage kids back in Cape Town. He was still holding on.

I thought of Corinne, at home in Scotland. We had not been together long enough. I wondered if I would ever have sex again. It seemed an absurd thought. Such a long, long way from a warm bed and my girlfriend. A long way from anywhere, and anyone. It might be a journey too far.

There was little human noise in the raft now. Those that had been moaning or wailing had stopped. In the darkness Big Danie pulled Morné and Eugene close, trying to keep warm. Morné could feel Danie's chest racked by shivers. In the faint light of the bulbs on their shoulders, he could see Danie's giant hands shaking.

Three hours or so had passed. My mind was adrift, often empty. Suddenly, Bubbles' voice rang out across the raft. I was surprised because he had looked near to death just minutes before, but now he began roll-calling all the crew he could remember. There were sixteen of us in the raft when we boarded, seventeen once we'd hauled in Peinge. But by the time Bubbles started doing roll-calls there were fewer than seventeen names being yelled out.

'Bjorgvin, Bjorgvin, are you here?'

'Yes, Bubbles, I am here still.'

'Boetie?'

'Yes, Bubbles.'

'Kenny?'

No reply.

'Kenny?'

Maybe Kenny was just being quiet.

'Brian?'

'Yes, Skipper.'

'Eugene?'

'Yes, Skipper.'

'Trevor?'

The roll-calls went on. Three or four times Bubbles called out our names, and it helped. The effort to force words from our mouths, and to acknowledge Bubbles, shook us from an idle descent into unconsciousness. It was also a reminder that we were not alone. But sometimes people no longer answered. As the cold had penetrated deeper into my body from the frigid water, I had felt my mind become sluggish. Each thought and task was now painfully slow. Through the haze of hypothermia, I was sure that Bubbles' list was getting shorter.

I could feel something other than the rubber floor of the raft, under my feet and knees. My legs were numb, but I knew somehow that I was pressing down on limbs or torsos. I had the distinct feeling that they were no longer alive. I was kneeling on someone, but I couldn't bring myself to care, as long as they offered some support to keep me out of the frigid water.

Boetie had been behaving oddly at times in the raft. One minute discussing with me whether to swim to the other raft, and wailing hopelessly, or suggesting we get in the water the next. The stern gantry had hit him so hard, and we were all so cold, that these outbursts could be forgiven.

Bubbles reached the end of his most recent roll-call, and finished by calling out the name of his best friend.

'Boetie?'

No reply.

'Boetie? . . . Boetie?'

'He is dead, man,' said Hannes, 'Stop.'

19

15:55

Just ten miles off the southern coast of South Georgia, the *Northern Pride* had already quit fishing for the day. Andreas' years of experience told him that it was not worth fighting through such conditions. If there were any fish on the line, most of them would still be there tomorrow. All but two boats had made the same decision.

The seas had been so rough that the main line had parted while they were hauling. The deckhands tied a large buoy to the line still remaining in the water, so that they could retrieve it another day, then Andreas ordered them to cut it away.

Free of the distraction of fishing, Andreas concentrated on keeping the boat head on into the swells. The *Northern Pride* could dodge and turn more quickly without the hindrance of the line, and Andreas planned to sail to a bay on the south coast of the island for shelter. However, with the worst of the storm already upon them, he could only hold position; they would have to cope with the swells in open water. He called for his second-in-command, Luis. With a broken autopilot, they would take it in turns at the helm as they waited for the storm to pass through.

Magnus Johnson had seen the weather fax that morning. The isobars were packed so tightly together that they appeared as just one big black blob between South Georgia and South America. No longer needed on deck, he returned to his cabin once the fishing was finished. Hearing the dishes crashing to the floor in the galley,

Magnus reasoned that it was rough enough to merit lying in his bunk in his flotation deck-suit. Just in case.

Shortly before 16:00, Captain Andreas heard the HF radio from across the bridge of the *Northern Pride*. The voice on the other end was unmistakeable. After years fishing for the same company, he knew Bubbles' gruff South African tones well and could detect the tension in his voice.

Bubbles' Mayday gave the basics. The *Sudur Havid*'s pumps had failed, she had shipped waves and she was sinking. Now they were about to board the life-rafts and needed help. Position: 53°56′S, 041°30′W.

Andreas noted down the co-ordinates, taking care to ensure that every figure was clearly written and correct. But the *Northern Pride* was more than a hundred miles south-east of the *Sudur Havid*'s current position. They had moved south a week or so ago, after refuelling, in the hope of finding more fertile fishing grounds. Even in good conditions, this distance would take nine or ten hours at full steam. He looked out of the windows at the steel-grey swells and their crests above his bridge. At a conservative guess, it could take at least twenty hours now. The day was ending, and the light would soon be fading.

Ordinarily, Andreas would have set his course and opened up the *Pride*'s engines to steam north-west, as fast as possible. But they were battling to keep themselves upright and afloat. Assistance was not an option. He pitied anyone in a life-raft in these conditions.

On the bridge of the *Isla Camila*, Captain Ernesto Sandoval Agurto heard Bubbles' Mayday and wrote on the whiteboard:

Barque abandonar: 53°56′S, 041°30′W

He picked up the radio microphone to hail his sister-ship.

'*Isla Sofia, Isla Sofia* . . .'

The frantic Spanish voice heard on the *Sudur Havid* as she was sinking was actually Chilean, and belonged to Captain Sandoval.

At fifty-four metres and with a GRT of 653 tonnes, the *Isla Camila* was substantially larger than the *Sudur Havid* and probably almost twice her weight. Now registered in Punta Arenas, Chile, but built in Holland in 1972, she was old but capable. The pockmarks and drizzle of rust on her blue and white paintwork was proof of her hard-working life.

The *Isla Camila* had returned to the fishing grounds just two days before, after making a halfway landing in her home port of Punta Arenas. Eleven boats were fishing in the South Georgia region ('Fishery sub-area 48.3') but they were spread out over thousands of square miles of ocean, all around the island. Most of the boats kept themselves to themselves, trying not to give away their positions and catch information. Some may have been in port, landing fish or refuelling. The Falkland-based fisheries patrol vessel MV *Dorada* may or may not have been nearby, but to allow effective surveillance, she did not advertise her schedule or position.

Now, when he needed to know the most, Captain Sandoval had no idea of the location of these boats. When he tried to call them over the radio, some did not respond, possibly due to bad equipment or reception, but also because of the language barriers of such an international fishery.

Any fisherman working in such distant seas knows that, when it all goes wrong, there are no rescue services to be called upon. There are no lifeboats to respond to a Mayday, and no helicopters to lift a crew to safety. A distress flare fired high into the sky will most likely fade unnoticed. In the Southern Ocean, boats work hundreds or even thousands of miles from the nearest port, city or rescue service.

A boat's best chance lies with its competitors. A crew will

attempt to rescue an ailing rival in the knowledge that, one day, they too may find themselves needing to be rescued. No captain or deckhand would want to be on a sinking ship knowing that they had refused to help others in the past and were not deserving of help now. This was not a close-knit band of brothers; few of the crews had ever met at sea, let alone on land. A troubled boat would put their trust in the goodwill of strangers.

Sandoval finally managed to make contact with a few crews but none were nearby. The South African boats *Koryo Maru II* and *Arctic Fox I* were keen to help, but were too far away to provide assistance before morning. Both were over a hundred miles from our last known position and would have to steam through the night. The *Isla Camila*'s sister-ship, the *Isla Sofia*, was at a similar distance and would not be of use in a rescue.

Of all the boats in the Southern Ocean, the *Isla Camila* was the closest to the *Sudur Havid*'s last position, but she was still thirty-three miles away. While the Captain continued to issue calls for assistance, the crew attached a massive buoy to the half-hauled line and prepared to cut the ropes. This would free the *Isla Camila* to sprint towards the *Sudur Havid*'s final co-ordinates, and to whatever was left behind. It was still daylight.

Phil Marshall, the *Isla Camila*'s Observer, appeared on the bridge at this point. A quiet, unassuming Yorkshireman, Phil stood out among the South American crew with his pale skin and aquiline nose. He had been on board the *Isla Camila* for five months, but had not been enjoying his time.

Phil noticed that something was wrong immediately. There were four officers on the bridge instead of the usual one and his eye caught the phrase on the whiteboard: 'Barque abandonar'.

'Oh my God, we're sinking?'

He turned to ask what was happening and saw the crew wrestling with the massive buoy, struggling to attach it to the fishing line.

'What's happening, Ernesto?' he pointed at the whiteboard, *'Que pasa?'*

For the next three hours the crew of the *Isla Camila* pushed the boat as hard as they dared, crashing south-east on a bearing of 117° through the furious seas. The Chief Engineer of the boat watched the gauges of the engine carefully and listened. While the engine worked at much lower revs than the screaming diesel of the *Sudur Havid*, a peculiarity of its long-stroke design, it was roaring now, and the noise in the engine room was deafening. He prayed that it wouldn't fail as the boat was pounded by the swells, and that all his cautious maintenance would pay off.

Captain Sandoval and the officers planned their search, and began readying the equipment and the crew. The journey to the stricken vessel's last reported position should take three and a half hours and, taking the Force 7 wind and ocean currents into consideration, they plotted where they would begin the hunt. Crew members ran between cabins and various stores around the boat. Binoculars, searchlights, grappling hooks, ropes, first aid kits and parachute flares were grabbed in armfuls, and spares were dug out from storage lockers. Stretchers, spare clothes and thermals were piled up in preparation. The Chilean fishermen changed into thick layers of jumpers, coats, hats and gloves, and put their oilskins and boots back on to keep the freezing wind and spray at bay. Taking into account the wind chill factor, they could expect −15°C on deck. They knew the search could take hours, and that they could expect to be outside the entire time, directing spotlights and peering into the darkness.

Old rope ladders were hauled out from the store and reels of weathered timber steps and thick faded rope were dragged across the boat. The crew tied the ladders to the railings on the top deck, but kept them rolled up on board, ready to be deployed.

Captain Sandoval tried to raise the *Sudur Havid* on the VHF and HF radios, but there was no response. Realizing that the other communications equipment was unoccupied, Phil offered to help. Maybe he could let the authorities know? In Spanish, he heard the Fishing Master, Paco, and Captain Sandoval bicker.

'Keep that Observer away from the radio!'

'This is my ship, I am the Captain. Everyone in South Georgia speaks English; Phil speaks English. We have to let him call them.'

Phil was finally allowed to make the HF radio call that would alert the rest of the world to what was happening. He first called Gordon Liddle, the South Georgia Harbour Master. Gordon bombarded Phil with a series of questions. How many have drowned, how many are injured? Phil's answer was short and to the point.

'We only know the latitude and longitude, I've told you as much as I can and that's the situation.'

At least now someone in a position of authority knew what had occurred and could contact others. But the *Sudur Havid* was too far from anywhere for anyone else to help. The few Royal Engineers 200 miles away on South Georgia had only small inshore boats, and the nearest helicopters were 700 miles away in the Falklands, far out of range.

Captain Sandoval watched the sea as they arrived at the *Sudur Havid*'s last reported position, hoping that some wreckage would appear in the floodlights. If the survivors were using a SART, a radio transmitter with an antenna, then a line of dots would show up on his radar display to guide them to its location. Nothing was showing up on the radar, neither SART nor ship.

On his command, the crew fired two parachute flares. The red lights arced high into the night sky and fell slowly under the billowing canopies, but any hope of illuminating the search area was quickly lost. Snow was now falling and, combined with the seven-metre-high waves, much of the light was obscured. The crew could not see any sign of wreckage or survivors, and the flares soon faded.

*

Back on the *Northern Pride*, Magnus returned from his bunk to find the officers all on the bridge. They were upset and worried about the *Sudur Havid*, but still faced the threat of the conditions around themselves. Andreas and Luis took turns at the helm, trying to keep the boat pointing in the right direction. They stared silently out of the wheelhouse windows and followed the meagre beams cast ahead by the floodlights. They tried to guess from which direction the next massive swell would come.

Magnus stood with his back braced against the wall. Through the windows he could not see the tops of the encroaching waves. The spray was so dense that it was hard to see even to the end of the boat, and unbroken waves were engulfing the bow every few minutes. The concentration and stress was clear on Andreas' face. The silence was broken only by cursing, when he was surprised by a swell coming at the boat from an unexpected direction. In all his time at sea, Magnus had never seen a Skipper work as hard as Andreas to keep a ship safe.

With no autopilot to maintain their course, it was also going to be a long night at the wheel for Andreas and Luis. Magnus picked up the radio microphone, and tried one more time to get an answer from the *Sudur Havid*, or the Harbour Master on South Georgia. He got no reply. All he could hear was broken-up speech and radio interference.

20

19:00

I waited. For morning, for rescue, for relief. Bubbles' roll-calls had wakened me from my stupor several times, but the intervals were growing and the cold was tightening its grip on me. I shifted my weight on the rope, and forced my hand further behind the pillar. Although my hands were numb, I could feel a piercing soreness in my fingers as the fabric of the canopy rubbed against them.

Trevor floated just a few feet away in the water. We had laughed together on deck that morning as he was drenched by the waves. Now, in the fury of the storm, he looked serene. His eyes were closed and the collar of his lifejacket gently cradled his head, pushing his bushy beard up to hide his mouth. The light on his shoulder still shone but his face had drained of colour. In the gloom of the raft, his skin was grey.

My eyes scanned over the rest of his body. His arms were relaxed and his hands floated loosely by his sides in a pair of my own orange gloves. He still owed me a haircut for those. Now he looked peaceful, drifting in the water. I knew he was dead.

The raft was contorting. Buffeted by the waves and the immense weight of the water that we were carrying, the vessel morphed from round to oval, from oval to round. The tubes around the edge were soft; they must have been losing pressure. Thrown towards each other from side to side, I wondered if we would capsize. There seemed to be nothing we could do to stop this, and if the raft flipped, we wouldn't be able to right it or climb back aboard. Hours of immersion in cold water had knocked the fight out of us.

I leant forward on the rope I was astride it, shifting to get more comfortable. In the faint light I saw a hand, loose around the rope next to me. The fingers were open, not gripping. Even through the haze of my hypothermia, it seemed too sad and futile. I reached down and closed the fingers.

They moved. I had assumed the hand belonged to one of the bodies submerged beneath the water, long dead, but I had clearly been wrong. Startled, I looked up along the line of the arm and discovered that the fingers belonged to Big Danie. He looked at me, confused, wondering what I was doing to his hand. No words were spoken. I shifted back on the rope, and returned to my wait.

On the other side of the raft, Morné didn't know what to do. It was dark, he was deep in the water and he was achingly cold; he couldn't see a rescue happening. Fumbling around his wrist, he felt for the silver bracelet that his girlfriend, Lee, had given him before he left. He kissed it and said goodbye. He had made his peace.

'Help me.' Eugene's voice broke the silence, thin and wavering. 'Somebody help me, please!'

I didn't know if he was calling for us, for God, or for a guardian angel, but I couldn't summon the strength, or find the motivation, to answer his call.

Time drifted by. A few minutes, maybe half an hour, then another request:

'Matt, can you give me a hand, please?'

A peculiarly polite appeal, for such a time. Hannes was once again struggling to do up the flaps that covered the doors of the raft.

'I can't, man, I'm stuck.' In a tangle of lifejacket ties, I felt the lines holding me tight around my lower legs and ankles. I also didn't want to leave my position. If I could stay here, perched on the rope and protected from the wind, maybe I could survive the night. In my deck-suit, maybe I stood a chance?

Eventually, ashamed at my unwillingness to help, my conscience kicked in and I released my hold on the pillar. I extricated my legs, moving them clumsily back and forth to free myself, and forced myself off my rope. I could feel that my body and mind had slowed – the cold was starting to affect me more and more. I was not in pain, but I had stopped shivering.

Slumping down into the water, I used my elbows to roll on to my stomach, and crawled stiffly forward. Each movement became a battle to force sleeping arms and legs to function. I pulled myself across the raft towards Hannes, who was lying next to the door. I was so tired. My feet and legs were numb, but I could feel objects bumping against me as I moved. Beneath me, lights glowed up from the water, dim orbs of light with a macabre twist; these were the lifejacket lights attached to submerged bodies.

Kneeling next to Hannes, I could feel that I was balanced not on the floor of the raft, but on the corpses of colleagues. If they were alive, they would surely have complained, but I was too cold to care.

Our frost-bitten fingers tugged at the canopy, and we tried one more time to thread the Velcro strap through the eyelet and down on to the corresponding patch on the tube. The task was more difficult now but it was more crucial than ever; we had to preserve the little heat we had left, if we were to survive. Blessedly, it gave my mind a focus: something I could achieve; something to stop me from dying. My frozen fingers worked to grip the strap like chopsticks, forcing it by sheer willpower through the eyelet. But our efforts only lasted seconds. The cover was ripped back from our fingers by the wind, and once again I was staring out at the icy abyss of the Southern Ocean. The cold air blasted in, and I shrank back. I tried to grab the flailing canvas, but my arms were too slow. And then there was a red light.

Good grief, was I imagining things? My mind was as slow as syrup as I tried to work out what had just happened. I knew I had seen something, but I couldn't make sense of it. Leaning on the tubes of the raft, I gazed out into the night. Like waking suddenly from a deep sleep, my brain tried to catch up with my eyes and with the sense that this was something important, and not to be missed. Was it a flare? Was it the other raft sending up a distress signal? I was jealous – where were ours? Or was it a boat?

While the cogs of my mind clunked slowly, the swells moved again and a wave dropped from our view, revealing again the image I had seen: a red light, and now a row of white lights below. It was the side of a boat, one hundred metres away, aglow with glorious illuminated bulbs. I glimpsed a red masthead and what appeared to be navigation lights; we must be to her port side.

'Lights!' I called out, simply. 'I can see lights . . . I think?'

Hannes looked up, and the others behind us in the raft stirred from their waiting and reveries. They began to search, too, for whatever I was seeing.

Had I reached the end of my tether? Was I hallucinating? I found myself gazing at the bright spotlights and deck lights of a boat, broadside to us, white against the night sky and black sea. Momentarily a spotlight near the bow confused me. Were there two boats now? What luck.

After hours in the raft, we had all slowed down. Our actions had become sluggish, and our reaction times were delayed. Our attempts to ensure our survival had become less and less frequent, and we had slipped into hushed suspension. Now, the prospect of imminent rescue forced our minds to fire up again. The adrenaline surged, there was no way we could let this chance slip away.

I yelled as loud as my lungs would allow.

'Over here! Help! Over here!'

I knelt at the edge of the raft and waved my arms. They had to be here for us, I thought.

'Come on, guys, there's a boat! We need to shout!'

Slowly, as my raft-mates realized that what I was seeing was not an illusion, they joined in and the chorus rose. We screamed our lungs out.

21

19:10

Captain Sandoval called the *Sudur Havid* again on the radio, and listened for VHF transmissions, but heard no reply. There was still no wreckage of the boat visible and nothing solid was showing up on the radar, apart from the temporary blips of mountainous swells. The ship must have sunk.

He turned on the beacon finder, usually reserved for locating radio buoys on the fishing line, in the hope that a rescue transponder or an EPIRB might show up. They would now be searching for life-rafts and for survivors. If the crew had stayed on the boat for as long as possible, as he knew they should have done, they would be close by downwind. But if they had boarded the rafts, or had been forced into the water, they would have been at the mercy of thirty-knot winds, vast swells and powerful currents for over three hours. The crew of the *Sudur Havid* could be spread out over an area of several square miles.

Trying to predict the complex interplay between the wind pushing any floating objects south-east, and the currents dragging them north-east, Captain Sandoval and his officers settled on a course of 080°.

The crew, manning their posts around the perimeter of the boat, were lashed by wind and spray as they scanned the ocean for any glimpse of a manmade object. Despite the aid of the searchlights, the poor conditions and visibility meant that it was almost impossible to spot anything in the water. With the *Isla Camila* searching alone, the urge to cover the grounds as quickly as possible had to be balanced with the need to be thorough, and progress slowed to just a few knots.

The race to the scene had been relentless as the *Isla Camila* beat its way through the waves. Now, with the engines slowed and the swells moving through, the boat rolled and yawed. A few of the deckhands climbed up on to the wheelhouse roof, hoping the extra few metres of height would offer a better vantage point, and braced themselves against the railings. The beams of the searchlights reached out into the night, highlighting the spray as it swept from the crests, and the snow as it swirled. Windswept droplets landed on the lenses of the few pairs of binoculars being used. It was only possible to see a few hundred metres on either side of the boat now and the crew had to scan slowly. The swells rose and blocked the lights, then dropped suddenly to reveal an entirely new vista. A whole ship could be hidden in the trough of a swell, let alone a life-raft.

19:30, Position: 53°55′S 041°24′W

Thirty minutes into the search and more than four miles from the last known position of the *Sudur Havid*, one of the deck crew at the rail started waving his arms frantically. He had glimpsed a flashing light. Paco turned the boat to follow the pointing arm of his colleague, heading slowly towards the intermittent pinprick of silver light. The searchlights mounted on the wheelhouse roof and mast illuminated the shifting water ahead. Suddenly, amid all the grey water and white foam, they picked out the fluorescent orange roof of a life-raft.

Paco deliberately steered away from the raft as it came close, before turning back to head into the wind. A fast downwind approach risked over-running the target and crushing them. Just as if he were collecting a buoy from a fishing line, he manoeuvred the boat upwind and brought it slowly alongside the raft. His fine and practised adjustments to the tiller and throttle kept the huge boat as steady as possible against the swells. The wind kept the raft close.

Although the *Isla Camila* was a long-liner like the *Sudur Havid*, her line and the fish were brought aboard through a more sheltered hatch positioned higher in the hull, about two metres above the waterline, on the starboard side. This was the best point on the boat from which to mount a rescue but the timing would be crucial – the rise of the swell would have to be judged to perfection to lift the raft close enough to the boat. With swells seven metres in height, or more, the raft would drop down the side of the boat. A fall from that height could easily result in injury or the casualty being pinned underneath the boat.

Normal training scenarios are designed for the recovery of a single man lost overboard. On this night, the potential numbers involved, combined with the weather conditions, raised the complications and danger immeasurably.

Five of the crew waited nervously at the hatch. More waited on the deck above. One of the men held a rusted metal grapnel hook, ready to throw. They had wrapped its four sharp points in scraps of fishing net to avoid hurting any survivors or damaging a raft. Ropes were coiled at their feet, in case casualties needed to be hoisted. The wooden rescue ladders were now rolled out and draped over the edge of the boat either side of the hatch.

When the raft came alongside, the crew at the hatch steeled themselves and called out.

Through the continuous howl of the wind, and between the occasional noise of the chops rolling in, Stephan thought he could hear something. A low throbbing sound, it was different from the others. Could it be an engine? Straining to hear against the background clamour, he wanted to be sure he was not imagining the noise. Light abruptly flooded the raft and the interior took on a sunset radiance. A searchlight had hit the canopy.

'There's a boat outside,' Stephan shouted. 'We must get to the boat!'

Charlie ripped open the door to be met with a blinding spotlight. Locked on the raft, barely wavering, the beam reassured him. They were just thirty metres away. There would be nothing worse than watching a potential rescuer disappear into the distance, still searching, but now he knew they were coming to help. He waved his arms, just to make sure.

With unexpected speed, the boat was alongside them in moments and the raft was battered against its side by the wind and the waves. Sven watched the rusted steel roll towards them – after hours of being tossed around by waves, the boat now threatened to crush or capsize them. With the ship to leeward, the wind blew them against the hull, bouncing the raft along its blue side. A rope and plank ladder came into view, hanging over the railing of the deck. Figures in orange-and-yellow oilskins stood on the top deck waiting to help them. Other rescuers were already gathered at a lower hatch in the side of the boat. The ship's crew had their arms outstretched, their hands poised to grasp.

Sven felt the raft rising up on the swell and the air around him was suddenly full of noise. He could hear voices yelling over the commotion of the water and the din of the engine. The crew were shouting at him, but he couldn't understand them. The raft dropped back down the side of the boat. He was on the wrong side of the raft to enter the lower hatch, but the ladder was still close to him. There was no point trying to climb up now; better to time it right. When the raft lifted up again, Sven saw his chance and grabbed the ladder as high as he could; his fingers were just strong enough to close around the rope. The raft fell away beneath him and he kicked his feet on to the broad wooden rungs of the ladder. He felt a flurry of hands gripping his freezer suit, pulling him up towards the metal railing.

Down in the raft, Stephan was ready to move. He had shaken off the lethargy of the cold but many of his raft-mates were not so fortunate. While a few were still alert and capable, others were sitting and staring, unable to move their stiff limbs or to revive their clouded minds. Watching the more able begin to climb the ladder, or be lifted to safety from the canvas entrance, Stephan grabbed the shell-shocked and helped them across the raft. Seeing that Gideon was almost unconscious, he teamed up with Charlie and pulled him by the arms to the opening in the canvas. Pausing to time the next move, when the boat rolled over them and the raft lifted, they heaved him up towards the ladder and into the saving hands reaching down from above.

A few moments later, Stephan looked around him: the raft was now empty. Everyone was safely off, on to the boat above. He looked up for help, but the figures were gone.

'Hey! I'm still here!' he called. Had they missed him? Surely they wouldn't sail away and leave him adrift?

'Hey! Hey! I'm here!'

The boat lurched towards him and Stephan realized this could be his only chance. He flung his arms over the railings. His hands were barely working but he held the railing tight under his armpits and clenched it to his chest. The raft fell away and he was left dangling, metres above the raging sea. The waves surged up beneath him. He cried out for help.

22

19:35

The brightly lit boat was disappearing behind the swells and I knew that our raft would be doing the same. Although we had no light on top of our life-raft, I thought maybe we could use the bulbs on our lifejackets to improve our chances of being seen. I had long since torn my own vest off – the strings had loosened and hog-tied my legs – so I reached for another in the water. Ripping the light from its clips, I swung it by its cables over my head, shouting as loud as possible to attract attention.

The light went off, just seconds after I lifted it up. I stared at the unlit bulb, trying to understand. *Of course* – they only worked when the contacts at the bottom were immersed in saltwater.

Reaching down to hold the bottom of the cable in the water, I whirled the top of the light around, now just inches above the surface. Thankfully, it worked. Small and weak though this firefly of light may have been, I hoped that it would reach out across the waves and be enough to stand out against the black of the Southern Ocean night.

The light slipped from my numb fingers and into the water. I fumbled for another only to fling it, too, out into the sea. Each time, I scrambled for another lifejacket from inside the raft, gripped the new light in my clumsy fist, and waved it back and forth above the water's edge.

Scared witless in case we were missed, I knew that a few minutes of intense effort might make all the difference.

'Come on, guys, yell! Yell so they can hear us!'

Forcing my useless hand into the left chest pocket of my deck-suit, I couldn't feel a thing but used my fingers to snag the cord that was tied to the loop inside. The whistle, attached to the cord, came out as I had hoped. Putting it to my lips I blew until it stopped whistling. When it stopped I howled at the top of my voice, and then blew some more. The rest of the guys were now shouting from the raft too.

'Over here! Over here!'

The boat turned towards us. It wasn't jubilation that I felt – I was too tired and numb – but the last embers of hope flared up inside me.

Even though it appeared that the boat was just moments away, the sensation or fear of warmth being stripped from our bodies was impossible to ignore. We ducked back inside the raft and closed the canopy door to block the freezing wind. Hannes and I jammed our heads through the slit that was left, desperate to check that the boat was still coming, then hid back inside again. We were just fifty metres apart now.

Back on the *Isla Camila*, Paco tried to keep the boat steady for the rescue from the first raft. One by one, the men were seized by their clothing or a rope was looped under their shoulders and they were hauled on board.

The boat was a scene of pandemonium. Out on deck, the crew were yelling instructions and requests, while the men on the raft were calling for help. Inside the bridge, everyone was talking at once and the communications equipment was alive with ringing phones, blinking lights and radio chatter. Amid all the confusion, another cry rang out.

One of the deck crew at the railing had spotted something: a flash of silver reflective tape, caught in the beam of a searchlight. It was another life-raft. With no lights, it was barely visible through the waves and the spray. After three and a half hours of drifting and ocean bombardment, the two rafts were separated by just seventy, maybe a hundred, metres. The crew were surprised to find the first raft so quickly. To find the second raft so close, unlit, was miraculous.

With no strobe aboard that raft to mark its position, it was imperative that the *Isla Camila* kept the new survivors in sight. Once the men were recovered from the first raft, Captain Sandoval ordered their vessel to be hauled aboard to avoid confusion. Paco turned the *Isla Camila* and gave a burst of throttle. The ship rolled as she went broadside to the swells.

Drawing closer, Phil could see that the second raft sat much lower in the water. He ran down from the bridge to the fishing hatch and leant over the metal railing, hoping to help in another triumphant rescue. When he had first glimpsed the previous raft, grateful faces had smiled back up at him from a mostly dry interior. This raft, however, was sagging and barely afloat; the canopy was still closed.

The low rumble of an engine was joined by the drum-thud of steel slamming down on to water. The new noises signalled that we could rip back the doors. The boat had arrived. The hull was massive, and loomed over our flimsy craft. The powerful lights shone down, ending the twilight in an instant.

The swell seemed determined to throw us under the hull. Ricocheting along the side of the *Isla Camila*, I could see crew spread out along the deck rail and in the fishing pit in vivid orange-and-yellow oilskins. Silhouetted by a halo of light, their faces were hidden in hoods, but I could hear their voices. Although a rope and plank ladder dangled down the side of the boat, the hull towered above us and the main deck seemed impossibly high. Even with my mind dimmed by hypothermia it was obvious that grasping and climbing a ladder with numb, weakened hands would be impossible.

The sea moved us away, and we were suddenly six metres from the boat. After so long in the raft, and after so much had happened, I was damned sure we weren't going to be lost to drift away. Driven closer to the gaffing pit on a rising wave, the crew threw a white rope towards us, which landed with a slap across the roof. I knelt up and stretched to grasp it but I was too slow; it slid into the water.

The second throw tangled on my stiff splayed fingers. I tried to hold on so that they could pull us in: if we could get alongside, we would all be able to board safely. I knew my crewmates were just behind me and didn't want to let them down. As I searched for something to tie the rope around, the raft suddenly shunted away from the boat. I watched as the rope ran through my fingers, slipping through my feeble, uncooperative hands. I was glad I hadn't tried the rope ladder.

On the next throw, the rope came free from *their* fingers and I was left holding the end. I looked at it, blankly. What the hell was I supposed to do with this? Throw it back? Whatever instructions our rescuers were yelling, I couldn't understand a word.

The *Isla Camila* was rolling up and down next to us and her metal hull threatened to crush us under the water as we bobbed up and dropped away on the swells. In seconds, we were lifted almost level with the crew as they stood in the line-hauling pit, until the water plunged us so far down her side that I could actually see the hull curve away towards the keel. I was suddenly staring at the underside of an 800-tonne boat; I knew that we could be obliterated at any moment. After fighting to survive for so long, our raft was in the most danger since we had been blown clear of the *Sudur Havid*. Our vulnerability was terrifying, and I felt powerless. Hannes was next to me, bawling 'Help!' Help!', but his hands and arms were as useless as mine.

Across the raft, a grappling hook landed next to Morné. Worried it would puncture the rubber, he dropped it in David's lap.

'Hold this,' he stammered. Clumsily, he formed a loop of rope and tried to feed it under the cord inside the raft. Before he could secure the knot, he felt hands grasping him. His lifejacket went tight around his chest and he was hoisted upwards.

After a few more hopeless attempts at grasping the rope being thrown to me, I gave up trying to help the rest of the raft and thought selfishly. I wasn't about to lose this chance of rescue. I held out my stiff arms, like a child reaching up for a parent's embrace. If I couldn't hold on to their ropes, they could hold on to me.

On the next swell, the raft was swept back up the side of the boat to within touching distance of the deck. My arms were raised but I couldn't quite reach the clutching hands above me. Moments later, on another swell, I was high enough to be briefly clasped, but my arms slipped through their fingers.

Third time lucky. A swell lifted us higher than any of the others and with my hands extended as far as I could reach, we ascended up the side of the blue and white hull. Two or three men leant out from the line-hauling pit and seized fistfuls of my deck-suit at the shoulders and arms. I felt their arms against my head as they raised me upwards, and my chest pressed against the metal plating of the hull. The raft dropped away, to leave me suspended over a long drop into the black water below. I yelled at my rescuers: 'Pull! Pull! Pull!'

For a few long moments I was treading on air, as though scrabbling for a hold. I would not rejoin my crewmates in the raft; I could not fall into the wild water below. My face was crushed against their colourful oilskins. A cacophony of noise and voices filled my ears.

Finally, mercifully, the fishermen pulled me over the railing and put me on my feet. My legs crumpled and I fell flat on my face on the cold, hard deck.

'Thank God.'

FOUR

DELIVERANCE

19:35

Illuminated in the harsh glare of the *Isla Camila*'s work lights, the flooded bowels of the second raft came grimly into focus. Phil shuddered. After years of service with the Whitby lifeboat, he was used to the sight of death, but it was the state of the survivors that shocked him. Those within were lying awkwardly: a knotted melee of arms, legs and heads floated in the water, and the odd foot or hand protruded from the surface, or was caught in a twisted web of lifejackets and ropes.

Full of water, and sitting lower in the waves, the second raft was going to be much more challenging to recover. Phil's fellow deckhands began throwing ropes to those inside, but their arms weren't working; the men in the raft seemed to be frozen from the shoulders down. A few casualties came within reach, and were hoicked over the side of the boat. Others waited in the raft, their arms outstretched in a desperate plea for rescue. They were unable to help themselves.

Phil found a rope and tied a bowline to make a loop, gesturing to his crewmates to do the same and to lasso over their shoulders. When a man was hoisted out in this way, it looked painful but there was no other alternative. He counted seven men alive, some almost unconscious. Many more remained in the raft, inert.

Once the survivors had been hauled aboard, the crew of the *Isla Camila* faced the problem of recovering the inactive bodies, which were either comatose or already dead. It was not as if those pulled first from the raft could have helped with the rescue, but now there was no one left to respond to a rope or a call. Due to the flooding, the raft was too heavy to lift. In the few minutes the raft had been alongside, Phil knew that some bodies had already been lost into the open sea. They watched as a ferocious wave crashed through the open doors of the raft, and washed out some of the limp corpses. Even with the powerful lights over the fishing pit, the bodies were soon gone into the night and the ink-dark water.

Phil and his crewmates coiled their ropes, and threw down the loops in an attempt to snag any limbs they could see, but many of the bodies were face down in the water. Their arms and legs were submerged, and the coils of rope floated uselessly on the surface. Phil watched as another wave swept through the raft, tumbling another body into the sea. With no lifejacket, it was gone in an instant.

When they managed to lasso a leg, it took three men to haul the body upside down out of the raft. The socked foot came over the railing first, and the deckhands shifted their grip to pull the man aboard. He thudded lifelessly to the deck, and they hauled him into the shelter of the factory deck.

Phil thought about tying a line around his waist and descending into the raft, but he couldn't embark on such a rescue bid without Captain Sandoval's permission. Besides, in such heavy seas, and without proper rescue equipment, such a tactic would be reckless.

Working in extreme conditions, and confronted with the risk of more bodies being lost from the raft, the officers and crew made a brave decision: they would use gaffs to retrieve the few bodies remaining. There was no sign of life and, judging by their face-down posture, they were probably dead. It was a brutal option, but it was the only way. The boat needed to continue with its search. They reasoned that the families would rather have a body back than nothing at all.

The bamboo gaffs were soon passed down from the deck above,

each with its gleaming stainless hook. The fishermen weighed the three-metre gaffs in their hands. This was something they had never expected to have to do. If they were right, and the men had drowned, then the gaff would do them no more harm. They fished around in the raft, as it crashed in the swells, trying to snag the men's clothing. They hooked the lifejacket of one man. The fabric and ties looked as though they would rip as they strained to pull him up. For the last few bodies, without lifejackets, the practised upward jab of the gaff drove the hook through the oilskins, and pierced feet and limbs to give a secure lift. It took three fishermen each using a gaff to lift one body; just as with the biggest toothfish. The four bodies were dragged through to the factory deck to a store room. Blood from their wounds marked their torn oilskins.

No more corpses could be seen in the raft. If there had been any others, they must have been washed away. The crew threw a grappling hook into the vacated raft, and started to winch it up. The hydraulic drone of the windlass rose in pitch as the rope strained and tipped the raft. The rubber squealed as it tore, and water poured back into the sea.

The twenty-one survivors in the canteen were now providing important information: thirty-eight people had been aboard the *Sudur Havid*, and three rafts had been boarded. Where was the third life-raft?

24

19:40

The crew ran towards Stephan and heaved him over the rail. He was able to stand on his own, but the men supported him on their shoulders and carried him through the storm door to the factory deck. Inside the warmth of the boat, in an accommodation area next to some showers, they helped Stephan strip off his wet clothes. Around the room, others from his raft were in even more urgent need of the crew's attention. Sven looked confused, staring in a daze and leaning heavily on the fishermen as they removed his oilskins. Gideon was lying on the floor, barely conscious. He was almost completely unclothed, and his skin was grey. When two men dragged the teenager through to the showers, he hung listlessly between them.

Stephan turned down the crew's offer of a warm shower but accepted the blanket, wrapping it tightly around him. Stumbling through to the boat's canteen, he slumped on to a bench and was handed a mug of steaming hot coffee. He fixed his eyes on the mug, and willed it to stop shaking; he was shivering so much that he couldn't hold the drink without spilling it.

I was unable to stand. My mind was vaguely intact but, after three and a half hours submerged in the freezing raft, my legs weren't working. When my saviours pulled me aboard, and put me on my feet, I tried to mutter some words of thanks before I collapsed on my face on the cold metal deck.

In the mad rush of the rescue, and with the crew of the *Isla Camila* eager to help other survivors from the raft, there was no time for tenderness. I was lifted under the arms by two crewmen, and dragged through the corridors into a cold store room.

One man supported me as the other unzipped my suit and tugged it down around my waist. They laid me on the metal floor and yanked the suit off, then used scissors to cut away my snug oilskins. Layer by layer, my insulation was being stripped away and I begged them to stop.

'No, no, too cold . . .'

They took no notice of my protest. My freezer suit was off in a moment.

'I'm too cold . . . don't take my clothes.'

Once my jeans and thermals were ripped off, I was left almost naked. I felt pathetic.

Incapable of walking, I was hauled through the corridors of the strange new boat and into the showers. My mind started to fire once more as I remembered my first aid training from SCUBA diving. Casualties could be killed by shock if subjected to rapid rewarming. What were they doing?

But as they held me in the shower and I felt the warm water across my body, the heat felt like such a blessing. I no longer cared about the shock and reached around to turn the water dial up hotter. My legs were numb, but my arms and hands tingled. After a few moments more in the steaming shower I was roughly rubbed down with a towel, and carried through to the mess.

Familiar faces looked up at me as I entered. Klaus briefly held my eye, but didn't speak. Other survivors from the *Sudur Havid* were sat around on benches. They all looked so warm and comfortable. Everything, in fact, seemed so normal but I felt detached. There was noise around me, but I couldn't make out what was going on.

Laying me down on the end of a bench, the crewmen peeled off my wet underwear. I must have been returning to my senses because I felt embarrassed. Good job there was no one around who cared. My skin was blue. I lay back helpless, cold and overcome. The men rubbed me briskly, their strong hands vigorously kneading my arms, legs and chest, and chivvying my circulation. Hannes was dragged through and laid on the next bench along. He landed abruptly, with a thump, and groaned. He was conscious, but lay blinking.

The crew dressed me like a baby, bundling me into someone else's clothes – first a loose pair of navy jogging bottoms, and then a woolly jumper, which smelt unfamiliar as it was hauled over my head. They jammed my swelling feet into a pair of shoes so tight that my toes hurt even through the numbness. They were speaking a language I couldn't understand. Was it Spanish? Lifting me around to sit upright on the bench they wrapped me in a blanket. Nursing over, and with other casualties on the way, not to mention a search to continue, they left me with my shipwreck mates in the care of the cook.

I could hardly sit. I felt weak and was racked by shivering, juddering to my core. A hot coffee was thrust into my trembling hands and, thinking of the guidelines for treating shock, I tried to say, 'No, no, I don't want coffee!' I was petrified of worsening my condition. But my mouth seized up and the words wouldn't come out.

Sod it. I gave up and sipped it anyway.

All fourteen of the men who were in the first raft had survived, and were sat around me now, huddled on the benches at three or four different tables. Mark appeared to be in good shape. Klaus was mumbling and quivering. Gideon seemed shell-shocked, and sat shaking in silence.

One by one the rest of the survivors from my raft were brought into the canteen: Big Danie, Bjorgvin, Morné, Brian and Eugene. Some were in the same state as me and were lugged through on rescuers' shoulders and laid on benches. A few, like Big Danie, had rallied and were able to shuffle through unaided. There was no celebration or cheer; barely even a greeting broke the silence.

My mental arithmetic wasn't at full speed, but I knew that there had been more people in my raft than were being brought into the mess now. Brian was one of the last to be saved, and was carried into the room.

'They're taking bodies off the raft,' he slurred.

While we were warming up in the canteen, the crew of the *Isla Camila* was still trying to recover corpses.

I was so very cold, and was shivering uncontrollably; it occurred to me that I might never warm up. Stephan sat next to me on the bench and looked remarkably well to my hypothermic eyes. I'd hardly spoken to him before, but I decided to ask him a favour.

'Mate, give me a hug.'

Stephan wrapped his blanketed arm around me. His body heat slowly percolated through my dry clothes and began to warm my torso, which felt like an ice-block. The clock on the mess wall read 7.45 p.m. It might take me hours to stop shivering, but I knew the worst was over. I was alive.

The Chilean cook ran back and forth, serving welcome food and hot coffee. He paused for a moment to rub something like Deep Heat into our hands. I clumsily tore apart a pale bread roll, and dipped a piece into watery vegetable soup. Everything tasted different from Grunter's familiar fare on the *Sudur Havid*, but I was famished. The ointment began to penetrate into the tissues of my fingers, prickling and smarting.

The heat of the room gradually revived us, and we began to talk in stammered sentences under our breath; we didn't have the energy for idle conversation. Those from the first raft were more alert, and wanted to know the fates of their crewmates. Charlie sat up on the table facing the centre of the room and began to gently quiz those of us who had been on the second raft. Each of us had seen different people at different times. It felt like we were in group therapy. Bad news was respectfully broken, one person speaking at a time.

'Have you seen Kenny?' asked Charlie.

'He is dead, man,' Eugene said, without hesitation. 'I saw him go.'

I was most worried about Simon, our Steward. He was vulnerable and the sort of guy you wanted to look after. I hadn't seen him at all.

'He's dead.' Morné broke the news plainly. 'He was in our raft, Matt.'

I hadn't realized; I would have tried to help. That spare coat in my cabin might have saved him.

'What about Bubbles?' asked Mark. Bubbles had been roll-calling almost until the end. I was sure he was OK.

Bjorgvin spoke up. In the raft I had lost track of him and was somewhat surprised, given his age, that he was still alive. Haggard, and leaning with all of his weight on the table, he held his large hands together, interlocking his fingers. He couldn't stop them from shaking.

'Bubbles died . . . at the end.' Bjorgvin stuttered. 'Just when the ship arrived.' It was the first time many of the crew had heard him speak.

In the raft I knew that Trevor was dead, but it hadn't dawned on me that there were others too. When I felt their limbs and saw them lying peacefully, I had thought they were just quiet, or were waiting in limbo for resuscitation. Maybe I even unconsciously tried to shut them out. But it was of no consequence now. The reality was that they weren't coming back.

We sat in the canteen and waited for news of the third life-raft. It hadn't been seen since we abandoned ship. Joaquim and Carlos were certainly aboard, but no one was sure if anyone else was with them. Melvin, Alfie and Kelobi were all still missing, as was Brian's son, Grant, and Charlie's brother, Albert. Given the state that we ourselves had just been found in, we couldn't expect them to survive for much longer. If their raft was undamaged, they still had a chance. We hoped that they had just been blown further downwind. No one was willing to write off their chances yet, but an unspoken consensus was growing.

25

21:00

The four men lay on the metal floor in the store room. Phil knew that people could appear dead when they were cold due to their vital signs being slowed and suppressed. He checked the bodies for airways, breathing and circulation, and tried to resuscitate them with the help of the Chilean crew. There was no response, and no improvement in the men's condition.

Ideally, the deceased would be laid somewhere warm, but Captain Sandoval wanted to shield the survivors from any further distress, which meant keeping the bodies out of sight of the living quarters on the ship. Phil would need to identify them for legal purposes, but that could wait. He arranged them in the recovery position and covered them in blankets and towels before being called up to the bridge.

The *Isla Camila* continued on the same course for another hour, Captain Sandoval reasoning that a lightly loaded raft could have been blown even further from the scene. Eventually he turned the boat, to make a parallel run back towards the last reported position. The trace on the GPS screen looked like they were laying long lines. Although the crew were accustomed to working on deck, the extreme conditions worried Sandoval, and he reminded himself to rotate the men in the most exposed positions. They could be searching all night.

Voices from the Royal Air Force crackled over the radio from their base on the Falkland Islands. They explain that they had two

Hercules aircraft ready to search, and all they needed was a position. However, flying so far from their base, the planes would be towards the limit of their fuel range, with just a short time to search on-site before heading back to refill. The officers of the *Isla Camila* pointed out that the sky was pitch-black and the conditions were atrocious; in their opinion, it would be time wasted. The decision was made to delay the search until the following morning, when daylight and better weather would improve their chances.

The owners of the *Sudur Havid*, now aware of the drama unfolding, faxed the *Isla Camila* asking for an update and a list of the survivors and missing.

'I don't have time!' Captain Sandoval declared. 'Phil, you prepare it and I will sign!'

At midnight, Phil found us in the canteen huddled close together on the benches for warmth, and perched around the heavy varnished tables. He approached one of the crew who seemed more together than the others.

'I need your help. I just need to draw up a list of the survivors, and the names of those missing.'

'It may not be that simple,' Hannes replied.

'Don't mess me around. Nothing could be simpler!'

'Well, do you want their real names, or the names they were working under?'

Many of the factory workers, lacking proper work permits and offshore tickets, had borrowed or bought paperwork and some had been working aboard using false identities. If their real names were given now, and the fraud was revealed, people back at home stood to get into a lot of trouble. But if their false names were used instead, their families or loved ones might never discover their fates, or face delays or mistakes.

'Use the real names,' suggested Phil. 'We'll just deal with the survivors for now.'

Phil typed up the list and we corrected the spellings. With the stamp and the signature of Captain Sandoval, it was faxed through to the company offices in Cape Town. Twenty-one known survivors.

Late that night, as the adrenaline faded and exhaustion set in, we were offered the chance of a few hours' kip in a bunk. The large communal cabin was hushed as I was helped to a vacant berth, my legs still stiff and weak. I sat on the edge of the bed, and the Chilean crewman gently lifted my feet and pulled off my tight shoes. I slipped under the rough woollen blankets, and pulled them tight around my shoulders. The reading light above my head illuminated an assortment of photos pinned to the wooden panelling beside me. Beloved faces of family and friends from Chile beamed out. I reached up and turned off the light. My fingers were sore, but working again. The warmth generated by my chilled core was slowly building and I drifted off to sleep.

26

06:00 (09:00 local time)

Eight thousand miles from South Georgia, in a kitchen in Back-well, near Bristol, England, a 51-year-old woman was washing up her breakfast dishes. It was sunny outside, the start of another warm summer day. The telephone rang. It was early for a call on a Sunday, only a few minutes past nine, but she assumed it must be something about church. She was surprised to hear a South African accent on the line.

'Hello, is that Marion Lewis?'

'Yes, speaking.'

'My name is Sean Walker. I am calling on behalf of the company that owns the *Sudur Havid*. I believe we have your son, Matthew, aboard our boat?'

The line was very clear.

'Yes.'

'I'm calling to say that the boat was lost yesterday, in heavy seas.'

'Oh.'

'What I meant to say is that your son is OK. He's been picked up, but the boat has sunk.'

'Oh.'

'I'm sorry to have to tell you this news.'

'Do you know any more?'

'No, there is not much information, but I'll ring again later when we know more. Speak soon.'

Click.

Marion laid the phone down, and slumped down into a chair. The news didn't seem real. She had heard from Corinne only a few days ago that her son was alive and well. Now she was being told that there had been an accident. She tried to imagine what it would be like where he was, in the Southern Ocean, in winter.

Sean Walker put the receiver down and crossed another name from the list. The typed document, faxed over from the *Isla Camila*, recorded twenty-one known survivors. The names did not match with the ship's manifest, and he knew it would take some investigation before he would be able to contact all of the families.

He had been up all night. When news of the sinking reached him, he made his way down to the office at the waterfront in Cape Town. He guessed that the relatives would not have a clue yet about what had happened, but he wanted to be sure that they heard from him first, and not on the news. He worked till after sunrise to phone the next of kin; it was the first time Walker, who was in his late twenties, had ever had to make these calls. He knew most of the crew on board, and many were good friends. The comfortable office and hot coffee were far removed from the tragedy unfolding in the Southern Ocean.

It was simultaneously the best and the worst job in the world. When he broke the news to wives and mothers that their sons and husbands were alive, he could sense their shock, joy and relief. When he looked at the list of the missing, he knew it would mean devastation and grief. Most of the families would know what 'missing' really meant, but some had no inkling of how unlikely survival might be. The weather in Cape Town, let alone Namibia, did not lend itself to imagining the conditions of a Southern Ocean storm. Most of the fishermen had spared their families the worry of the true dangers of the trip before they left. The next number he dialled, to a mobile phone in Namibia, did not connect.

★

At a church in the Strand, on the outskirts of Cape Town, Mr Lizamore was attending his granddaughter's christening. Halfway through the service he felt a sudden urge to leave. He ran his hands through his unruly grey hair, trying to subdue the instinct that something was wrong, but he couldn't settle. Lizzie made his excuses to his wife and climbed into his pick-up to drive home. A few minutes later he arrived at his Cape Dutch house. He climbed the steps to the porch, and fumbled with his keys. The unease had not subsided. When he walked through the front door, the phone rang.

'Hello. Is that Mr Lizamore?'

'Hello, yes.'

'It's Sean Walker. Sven is OK.'

Lizzie burst into tears.

27

07:00

The search went on through the night. Exhausted and freezing, the crew of the *Isla Camila* remained out on deck for hours at a time exposed to the snow and the spray. Occasionally they took short breaks in the canteen and joined us for a hot drink and a bowl of soup. After months at sea, I imagine, the sight of our strange faces around their tables was disconcerting.

I had slept peacefully for a few hours, but then my bunk was needed and I had shuffled through to the canteen. I now knew the crew to be mostly Chilean; few, apart from Phil and the Argentinean Chief Engineer, spoke any English. I tried to make small talk, and confer our eternal thanks, but the conversation quickly stalled. Minutes later they were out on deck again, scanning for the missing third raft and any other survivors. We were in no fit state to help.

Daybreak made the search a little easier, and should bring the arrival of two new boats on the scene – both Cape Town long-liners. I remembered the *Koryo Maru II*, an elegant white long-liner that we had seen once before. Fifty metres in length and built in Japan, she rode the waves beautifully, Bubbles had commented, staying upright rather than rolling around. *Arctic Fox I* also arrived; a sturdy black and white converted stern trawler, built in Canada. They had both steamed through the night to offer their assistance.

Phil scanned the horizon with binoculars, but could not see either of the boats. They were showing up on radar and he could hear them on the radio. He tried to give them information on what had been found so far and pass on Captain Sandoval's advice regarding where to search. Other boats, still far away, were asking for updates, and crew and Observers were enlisted to translate between Spanish, English and Afrikaans.

Phil listened to some of the radio traffic with irritation. With no coastguard or rescue body stationed in the area it was unclear as to who was in charge. Even though the *Isla Camila* was on-site and had the best picture of events, Captain Sandoval was wary of dealing with the English-speaking authorities. Some of the boats were competing to take command, even though they were still miles away. Their constant radio talk was blocking up the airwaves. The *Northern Pride* was also motoring towards us and expected to arrive later in the day, but their HF radio was malfunctioning. Magnus kept calling to ascertain the situation and, when no one replied, he called again.

At 08:30 a small, light-grey shape was seen riding the waves by those on deck. The *Isla Camila* moved closer to inspect. It was the *Sudur Havid*'s inflatable boat, the 'rubber duck', that had been too heavy for us to lift off the deck. Free of the straps that once held it in its cradle, it had survived the night. Phil knew at once there would be no one aboard: the boat was sitting high in the water, and being blown around by the wind. Sure enough, when the dinghy came alongside, it was empty. Joaquim and Carlos, if they were alive, had to be in their own raft still.

The deckhands hooked it with a grapnel and hoisted it aboard. With so much of its bulk exposed to the wind, and so little weight or drag in the water, we calculated that this inflatable should have been blown further than most objects from the wreck. Unless there was a strong current, it seemed unlikely that anything would have drifted further away from the *Sudur Havid*'s final position than this.

★

Phil descended the two decks to the store room. There was a job he had been dreading. First, he checked the bodies' vital signs one final time, just in case one of them had flickered back to life. There was nothing – they were stiff and cold. Next, Hannes and Brian offered to identify the men. Phil had tried to make sure that they were laid out with some dignity, but Hannes and Brian were still visibly shaken as they gave names: Peinge, Kanime, Haimbodi and Jerimia.

On the advice of the maritime authorities in Chile, Captain Sandoval took the next logical step to preserve hygiene on board: the bodies were blast frozen. While a crewman watched at the door to prevent any of us from witnessing the process, the bodies were checked for possessions and then laid out on an aluminium tray. Phil told me it reminded him of the morgues he had seen on TV detective shows. Each body was slid into the racks of the massive freezers, which were normally used for the toothfish. Once frozen, they were wrapped in tarpaulin and stored in a bay of the hold.

10:00, Sunday, 7 June 1998

Dressed in a borrowed freezer suit, I wandered out on to the top deck of the *Isla Camila*. The wind had calmed somewhat to Force 5, which meant that it no longer tore the crests apart and the swells had decreased to six metres. The boat was pitching and rolling, but it was possible to lean against a railing and watch without fear of being thrown overboard.

I had a misplaced idea that I could help spot survivors, but I also needed a break from the intensity of the canteen. The deck provided thinking space, and the sea was familiar to me in a way that the new boat was not. Looking out from our new safe refuge, I was reminded how vast and featureless the search area was. How would anyone be able to see something as small as a raft or a drifting body?

I shifted my stance against the railing, to ease my painful feet. Watching the crew of the *Isla Camila*, I studied their clothes. They weren't just differently dressed, they were better dressed than us. Their chunky, thick-soled wellington boots, which had at first looked silly to me, offered insulation from the cold metal deck. Their oilskins were neatly belted in at their waists to seal out the draughts and spray. Each belt held a sheathed knife where it was needed: to hand. I knew that they would not have been caught as unprepared as we were.

I had heard that an aircraft would be searching the area, and I didn't have to wait long to see it. The drone of the engines gradually grew to a thunder as the heavy-bodied plane flew overhead. The Royal Air Force Hercules C130 aircraft had flown from its base on the Falklands. I guessed that it was still over a hundred metres in the air, but I could make out the blur of the four propellers against the low cloud. It provided a new perspective for the search.

Poor communications with the *Isla Camila* made the job of the aircrew more difficult than it needed to be. Although they had the *Sudur Havid*'s last reported position, they needed more information about the finds so far and the sea conditions overnight. Captain Sandoval seemed to misunderstand their questions, which hindered their search attempts. I watched the Hercules fly over, and then retreated into the warm canteen; they could be searching for hours. My fingers and toes ached too much, and the freezing wind was reminiscent of the raft. I couldn't stand the idea of being cold again.

A few floating objects left behind by the sunken vessel offered pinpoints of rare colour against the monotone grey ocean: buoys, lifejackets, clothing. Once the crew of the Hercules had spotted them, they relayed the positions of the debris to the fishing boats below, who, in turn, moved in to investigate. Seven hundred miles from its base, the Hercules would normally have had just a short time to search. Today, the crew arranged to refuel from a VC-10 aircraft, allowing them to stay on scene for longer. They searched further and further from us.

The *Koryo Maru II* approached a patch of debris reported by the crew of the Hercules. It was still not easy to locate the objects that had been seen. The shifting swells and the boat's low viewpoint meant that the crew could easily miss any objects in the water until they were almost on top of them. The body in the lifejacket was hard to miss, though – the orange collar of the vest moved up and down in the swells, beckoning the *Koryo Maru II* forward. News of the find came over the radio: the casualty had a gold tooth. It could only be Kenny.

11:30, Sunday, 7 June 1998

Back on the *Isla Camila* we moved closer towards the position of the *Koryo Maru II*. Phil heard a cry from on deck.

'*Cuerpo! Cuerpo muerto! Cuerpo!*'

Although he didn't speak much Spanish, he quickly figured out what it meant. Another body had been sighted. The orange life-jacket had been seen first, but the way the body lay so low in the water made it obvious that there was no hope of a survivor. A few giant petrels flapped away as Paco cautiously brought the boat next to the corpse. The face was pallid and had been damaged by the seabirds. The man's arms floated at the surface, his jumper rippling in the water. He was utterly lifeless and gaffs were used to bring him aboard. Hannes was asked to identify him. It was Bubbles: the last to die in our raft, he had drifted alone all night.

We had known that Bubbles was dead. News of his body being found was sad, but changed nothing. Hannes was almost back to his normal self, in the way he described the details.

'You should have seen his face, Matt, it was all damaged by the birds!'

The canteen was crowded with the crew of the *Isla Camila* try-ing to eat their normal meals, and there was nowhere else for us to be. Everyone was talking about what had happened and struggling to set their own record straight in their head. Not all the versions matched up.

Klaus was muttering about a big wave sinking the ship and was by far the most vocal on the subject. I was irritated that he seemed to be trying to embed his version of events. He had been asleep for much of the drama.

Alfius seemed to be obsessed with drying his documents; he had kept hold of his satchel, and was now laying the papers out and separating the damp pages. His lack of response to our pleas for assistance in the factory was still vivid in my memory.

13:00, Sunday, 7 June 1998

Arctic Fox I, searching a few miles from our location, homed in on a black shape they had seen, moving strangely in the swells. Orange fabric became visible underwater as they drew close. It was an upturned life-raft. The raft was completely flooded, and had collapsed. They hauled it aboard, and called in the find to Captain Sandoval. There was no one inside, and no sign of anyone nearby.

News of the recovery reached us in the canteen. We all knew what it meant. Eleven people were still 'missing' but with this discovery, it meant that they must all be in the water. We all knew just how bitterly cold the ocean was. Anyone adrift didn't stand a chance. The eleven missing were almost certainly dead.

For two of my crewmates, the news had grave implications. Brian cast his eyes down at the table. He had known that his son, Grant, was probably gone, but had held out hope that somehow he had made it to the third raft. Charlie was stoical, he didn't break down or sob, but he must have been devastated. He had to relinquish the last realistic chance of seeing his brother, Albert, alive again. An arm around a shoulder was all the support we could offer them.

This last raft to be recovered had been the first to flee the *Sudur Havid*. Joaquim and Carlos had boarded the raft and cut the line, letting it drift away with just a few people when it was built for twelve. We would never know who was aboard; it was maybe just the two of them.

I wished Joaquim and Carlos had survived to be able to argue back and inform me why they, who were supposed to be telling the crew what to do, chose to cut the rope and set the raft free long before the others. Maybe they were trying to rescue people who had drifted away from the boat. Maybe they panicked at the prospect of a fight for spaces. It felt like they were looking after themselves. Ironically, we suspected that it may have been because their raft was less heavily loaded that they were more vulnerable. Our raft was nearly overturned on several occasions, being blown around by the wind and buffeted by the swells; therefore a large raft with a smaller load was surely even more prone to capsize.

16:00, Sunday, 7 June 1998

It was twenty-four hours since Captain Sandoval had first received the Mayday call from the *Sudur Havid*. The boat was over capacity, carrying thirty-eight members of the *Isla Camila*'s crew, twenty-one of us rescued survivors and with five bodies packed aboard. The weather was still rough, and Captain Sandoval knew that if the boat got into trouble now, there would not be enough lifesaving equipment to go around. Other boats had arrived which could take over the search. With diminishing chances of finding anyone else alive, it was time for us to leave.

Captain Sandoval was worried about our physical and mental health and that we would start to show signs of nervous collapse as the adrenaline faded, or that we would suddenly deteriorate. Most obviously, our feet needed medical attention. Many of us, particularly the seven from the second raft, were experiencing the symptoms of 'immersion foot' as our feet and lower legs began to swell. Our skin had become tight, and the sensation had not returned, or was limited to tingling. Bjorgvin's feet were discoloured and still cold to the touch. His lack of circulation after a full day was of great concern and hinted at severe damage. Among the survivors, there were no broken bones or open wounds, no casualties lapsing in and out of consciousness and no unusual symptoms. It sounded obvious, but those who had died were dead, and the rest of us were alive. No one was in a critical condition.

The British Admiralty called on the satellite phone, demanding that Captain Sandoval take us to Stanley, in the Falkland Islands, where proper hospital facilities and an airstrip were available. Although Stanley was 700 miles away, and directly into the worst of the weather, the Admiralty reminded Sandoval that according to maritime law survivors should be taken to the nearest available port with 'appropriate medical facilities'.

The *Isla Camila*'s owners in Chile, meanwhile, were pressing their captain to put into South Georgia, just 200 miles away, and then resume fishing. This island, without proper medical amenities or even an airstrip, was ill-equipped to deal with us but at least we would be off the ship sooner.

Despite protests from the Admiralty, Captain Sandoval reasoned that he would never have to contend with them again whereas the vessel owners paid his wages. He chose South Georgia and we headed east, abandoning the search at 16:30.

Although we were sad to be turning our backs on the search, we owed everything to the crew of the *Isla Camila* and respected their decision. We knew that we had pushed our luck to survive as we did. The *Northern Pride* would stay in these waters for a few more days, co-ordinating the other vessels, who could continue to look for any signs of life, or to recover any more bodies that might console grieving families. They would find only boots, lifejackets and other odd objects floating around; scant evidence that a boat had ever even been there.

28

13:00

We were a ragged bunch, disembarking in the sheltered waters off King Edward Point, South Georgia. The island was home to just a Harbour Master, twenty Royal Engineers and an eccentric couple living on a yacht – all British. Gordon Liddle, the Scottish Harbour Master we contacted from the boat, didn't really want twenty-one unexpected guests in the middle of winter, or their medical problems, but he dutifully welcomed us.

Wearing borrowed underwear, freezer suits and shoes (our boots were most conspicuously missing), we waited for the Royal Engineers to ferry us to shore. The green Rigid Raiders that would carry us, five metres long and fitted with outboard engines, looked tiny after weeks on a metal fishing boat. We said our goodbyes to the *Isla Camila*'s crew. But how do you really show gratitude to someone for saving your life, particularly when you don't speak their language? Our words felt inadequate.

Phil packed his bags and came with us. He would also be travelling home. One at a time, we climbed awkwardly down the wooden ladders hanging from the *Isla Camila* – the same ladders that we had been unable to climb up from the raft. The boats could seat just six of us at a time, and the coxswains motored slowly across the calm water of the cove.

Low cloud hid the peaks, but the scenery was still magnificent. Winter had set in since our last visit in April, and the snow and ice had spread down from the mountains. The wind had scoured the frozen tracks between the few buildings, but snow gathered among the tussocks of grass and against each of the scruffy old sheds. The three-storey accommodation block, with its red corrugated roof, stood on a bluff just a few hundred metres from the quay. It was to be our home for the next few days.

When the Rigid Raiders pulled alongside the low concrete and stone quay at King Edward Point, in the shelter of the buildings, we were met by Gordon and a group of the Royal Engineers. The soldiers wore green-and-brown combat fatigues, which stood out against the snow and the stone that lay around them. They helped us out of the boats, and roughly shook our tingling hands.

The other survivors walked up to the accommodation block while Phil and I, in our role as Observers, were invited for a cup of tea and debrief with Gordon. The building nearest the quay was more freshly painted than the others, and this was his office. In the absurdly quaint and cosy room within, we sipped tea from china cups while Phil described the rescue. Gordon was smartly dressed in the same navy jumper with epaulettes that I remembered from our inspection, all those weeks before. He seemed more interested in talking to Phil than to me and I felt strangely ignored. I was bursting to tell my story of what had happened to the *Sudur Havid*, but they were concentrating on what had happened on the *Isla Camila*. Settling myself back into an old armchair, I let the conversation flow by me as I looked around at the wooden tables darkened with age, the faded prints on the wall and the threadbare rugs on the floor. It was a room from a bygone age, so different from the veneer and vinyl of the *Sudur Havid*. The room was quiet and still. I placed my teacup back on its saucer. For the first time in months, I did not have to worry about it falling over.

Tea finished, we made our way through the scattered buildings and shipping containers, towards the large green accommodation building. It was just a few hundred metres away, and I was eager to exercise my legs, but, with my feet swelling with tissue fluid, the journey was uncomfortable. Many of the old corrugated buildings of the settlement were boarded up, as though waiting for another community to restore them to their former glory. Towering above the village was an awe-inspiring backdrop of mountains, gullies and ridges picked out in snow and rock. I hadn't expected to return to South Georgia, at least not like this.

The building was home to the small unit of British armed forces year round through the sub-Antarctic winter and was sturdy and warm. As I shuffled up the steps and opened the door, I heard the familiar voices of my crewmates. Big Danie's and Hannes' booming tones were already ruining any peace and quiet. Then I was hit by the smell – glorious British fried food. Sausages, bacon and scrambled egg, all waiting to be devoured. The food Grunter produced on the boat had been good, but it always tasted different. Gorging myself on home comforts, I refuelled my exhausted body.

Quietly, while we were distracted by the warm food and the novelty of stable land, the Royal Engineers helped the crew of the *Isla Camila* move the five recovered bodies to shore. Still frozen and wrapped in canvas, the bodies would be kept in a metal container that acted as the base's meat store for the duration of our stay. The two life-rafts, deflated and trussed up, as well as the inflatable dinghy were also brought ashore.

Like the rest of my raft-mates, my hands were still sore and tingling; my feet were puffy and still lacked sensation. Fortunately, a pretty female medical officer made the treatment of our injuries more appealing; she was the first woman we had seen since the start of April. She injected us with antibiotics to counter any infection that might set in. The prick of the needle pierced through the numbness. We needed to keep our feet warm and clean, she explained, but other than that there was not much else that we could do. The warmth and space provided us with a chance to stretch our legs and shuffle around the lino floors in socks, like old people in a nursing home. We now had a few days to recuperate, without the distractions of civilization.

The first night brought unrest. However big the accommodation block had seemed from the outside, only three rooms were available for us to use, each with eight bunks. We were as cramped as we had been on the boat, and the initial bonhomie of the *Isla Camila* had gone. Then we had been catching our breath, relieved to be alive. Now, we had processed the events more in our minds. I claimed a bunk, only to find out that I was next to Klaus and Glen. I didn't want to be in the same room as people I held partly responsible for the sinking, but there was no choice.

Tuesday, 9 June 1998

The arrangements for the next stage of our journey home were confirmed. Although the 11,000-tonne tanker Royal Fleet Auxiliary *Gold Rover* usually transported fuel and supplies for the Royal Navy, she was the only available vessel big enough to carry us all to the Falkland Islands. She was already on her way and would arrive at King Edward Point on Thursday, weather permitting. The conditions had eased since the day of the sinking but Force 6 or 7 winds and six-metre swells were expected at the end of the week, possibly worse.

18:00, Tuesday, 9 June 1998

Our first phone call home. The British garrison had a satellite communication system and we would be allowed just three minutes each. I knew that there would be little point in phoning early in the day, as Corinne would be at work, so I let the others go first. The uncomfortable walk from the accommodation block down to the hut by the shore gave me barely enough time to plan out what to say. I waited in the porch of the hut while Hannes phoned his girlfriend in Cape Town. He wiped a tear from his eye when he came out. I dialled Corinne's number.

The phone was ringing.

There was no reply.

I was desperate to talk to her, to tell her that I was alive. But she wasn't there. I called my mum, in Bristol, instead. The words I always used to start our phone calls just slipped out.

'Hi, Mum, you all right?'

'I'm fine, son, but how are you?'

The line was crystal clear. She could have been in the next room. I wanted to tell her what had happened, how bad it had been and that we had nearly died, but I couldn't bring myself to upset her. I settled for reassurance. I told her that I was OK, that my feet were sore, that we didn't know when we would be home and I asked her to promise to contact Corinne. Three minutes wasn't enough.

'You wouldn't believe the size of the waves, Mum, the seas were horrendous.'

I paused.

'We didn't all make it.'

Wednesday, 10 June 1998

The 'residents' of South Georgia suggested that we should hold a memorial service before we left the island. They would erect permanent memorials, after our departure, but for now we were to lay a life-ring in the cemetery across the bay in Grytviken. It would help us to lay the dead to rest. We would hold the service the next day.

Celebrating the survivors, one of our lifejackets was installed in a more lively location – on the wall of the soldiers' bar, inside the accommodation block. We signed the lifejacket with our names: the ones that got away. For the rest of the evening we played Giant Jenga on the floor, and tried to drink the garrison clean out of alcohol. Hannes even gave Klaus a haircut. His hair had grown scruffy at sea and we would be back in the real world soon; our time as a crew was coming to an end. No one mentioned to him the discreet ponytail that Hannes had left behind.

Thursday, 11 June 1998

With our feet encased in thick socks and ill-fitting, borrowed shoes, we set off for the short boat trip across the bay to Grytviken. We could have walked, had it not been for the seals and the state of our feet.

Colossal elephant seals occupied the beach. In better times, I would be seeking close encounters with such wildlife, but none of us were in the mood to test our athletic shuffling skills against a few thousand pounds of irate blubber. Our feet were beginning to blister. The better our bodies and minds felt, the worse our feet had become, and most of us were now hobbling. Morné's legs and feet were so swollen that the skin was tearing apart. Bjorgvin's frostbite was so raw that he was told to stay at the garrison.

The Royal Engineers ferried us across the bay in their Rigid Raiders. At the dockside, waiting for the boats, we prodded at the slashed bundles which were all that remained of the life-rafts that had saved us. We couldn't believe that our lives really had depended upon such faded, ragged assemblies of rubber and cloth. The *Sudur Havid*'s inflatable dinghy lay forlornly next to them, its familiar grey rubber marked and scuffed, but still half inflated.

For a group of men who had just been shipwrecked, we were surprisingly carefree as we took to the water again on the small boats and whizzed across the bay. We even waved at the crew of the *Isla Camila*, who were still at anchor and waiting to return to fishing.

We climbed up the track to the graveyard on the hillside above Grytviken. Here lay sealers, whalers, submariners, explorers and heroes all resting together in peace. The granite headstone of Sir Ernest Shackleton jutted from the snow, which lay thick on the flat ground, hiding many of the other graves around us. A tall white cross stood proud on a cairn in the centre of the cemetery. We gathered around, and hooked our life-ring over the metal monument. We weren't ready to lay our friends to rest just yet, but knew that we would never have the chance to leave a memorial so close to their final resting place again.

After we had left for home, the life-ring would be mounted on the wall of the church in Grytviken, with a brass plaque bearing the names of the seventeen dead. One of the Royal Engineers, Corporal Martin-Stuart, had already planned a white wooden cross, which he would erect high on the hill above Grytviken. Their gestures were moving: our colleagues would be commemorated alongside Shackleton.

We paused for photos beside the life-ring on the cross. Phil had brought his camera, and one of the Royal Engineers took the pictures as we stood as a crew and in smaller groups of friends. It seemed wrong to smile.

Before we left the graveyard, we formed a circle next to the cross. I stood looking out over the bay. Grunter, acknowledged by all of us to be the most religious on board, was asked to say a prayer. Whether we agreed or disagreed, believed or not, we all bowed our heads. For once we were all listening and there were no distractions. No screaming winches, no seabirds and no Boetie yelling out of the window.

'Heavenly Father, Lord God Almighty, we are here today to commit our brothers to you.'

He went on, but the words grated. I remembered I had prayed in the raft, but Grunter was talking more about his caring God than about the men we had lost. Kashingola and Brian tried to pay their respects but trailed off, embarrassed. They were more used to the banter of the deck, and not familiar with expressing their heartfelt feelings in front of everyone watching. None of us were used to imparting words of such weight.

Below us, in the sheltered bay of King Edward Cove, the *Isla Camila* shifted at anchor, as the gusts flicked ripples into the calm water around her. It had gone quiet, and people were beginning to shuffle their feet in the snow. Hoping the tears would stay hidden in my eyes, I coughed to clear my throat and spoke up.

'I want to say something.'

Even in that moment, I still felt as though I was an outsider speaking at a private ceremony. Yet nothing had been said that expressed how I felt.

'Go ahead, Matt,' said Hannes, from around the circle.

I raised my voice, loud and clear, wanting my words to carry out to sea.

'There are three things I'll never forget about the *Sudur Havid*. One: the good times and the laughs we had on that boat, before the accident.'

I paused. People nodded.

'Two: the way people behaved on the day.' I took a breath, and looked down into the bay.

'And three: that boat out there, the *Isla Camila*, and the way they saved us.'

29

09:00

The RFA *Gold Rover* arrived in the night but, with rough weather and shallow water in the cove, she waited for us out in Cumberland Bay. It would be a one-kilometre ride in the Rigid Raiders to embark.

I could not see a way to board the huge tanker, but a cable dropped down, and the whole Rigid Raider was winched ten metres up into the air. We stepped aboard a very different vessel to the *Sudur Havid*. Even though the crew of the *Gold Rover* complained about the rough seas and bouncing off the corridor walls as they walked, it felt as still as dry land to us. Gone were the cramped crew cabins and the dingy mess room. Now we slept on camp beds in a huge cargo hold, ate well in a pristine canteen and drank beer in a comfortable saloon. We were dressed in identical navy-blue trousers and jumpers from emergency packs that were designed for refugees.

Only one person had survived the sinking with any real personal possessions: Alfius. Although a few men had grabbed their identity cards and mobile phones before we abandoned ship, Alfius had packed all of his documents into a briefcase, even when he should have been trying to start the pumps. It hadn't helped an already sensitive issue that Alfius had been so obvious in drying his papers on the *Isla Camila*. There was a certain lack of dignity in a man who fussed over his belongings while his comrades' bodies were still missing. Back on the *Sudur Havid* I had seen the brown leather satchel tied to his lifejacket as he waited in line to board the rafts, but it was so small that I decided against making anything of it at the time. On board the *Gold Rover*, his was the only bed with possessions on top. It turned out later that Glen had also managed to save his qualifications and paperwork, and placed them in Alfius' bag for safekeeping.

On the second night aboard the *Gold Rover* Alfius discovered that his case was missing. He came into the saloon as we were relaxing with a beer.

'Has anyone seen my briefcase?' he stammered.

I wish I had seen the bag as it was thrown from the deck. I wish I had thought of doing it myself. Hannes had found himself alone in the cargo hold. The satchel had been annoying him for days, and was lying on Alfius' bunk. He picked it up, and carried it out on deck. The floodlights above were illuminating the spray and the wash from the boat, as it motored through the night. Taking a step back from the railing, he flung the satchel out to sea, watching as the shiny leather spiralled off into the darkness. I'm glad that Hannes acted. His impulse made us all level; no one had anything except themselves.

Sunday, 14 June 1998

The journey aboard the *Gold Rover* allowed us to decompress. We had time to chat and drink beer, and our smiles returned. Sailing west, we crossed the Antarctic Convergence, leaving the frigid Antarctic waters behind us, along with the snow and the bitter winds of South Georgia. Although lonely and treeless, the Falkland Islands looked more like Scotland. When the *Gold Rover* docked at Port Stanley, we were one step nearer home.

We stayed at the British Antarctic Survey's hostel, just a few streets from the harbourside in Stanley. The friendly Falkland Islanders showed us the warm hospitality so often seen in remote places, and we soon found the Globe Tavern. With its dimly lit interior and dark wood bar and stools, it was built to exert a siren's call to mariners such as ourselves. We would be regulars for the next five days.

Tuesday, 16 June 1998

Bringing the bodies ashore in the Falkland Islands triggered the involvement of the Islands' Coroner, which meant a police interview for each of us and then a Coroner's Inquiry. Some of the crew had been told that this was just the British being bureaucratic, and that the shorter their statements, the sooner they would be free to return to South Africa. Eager to see their families, and wary of angering their bosses, some gave such short accounts that they were almost amusing in their brevity.

It would not help the police if all I said was 'My name is Matthew Lewis. I worked on the *Sudur Havid*. It sank on 6 June.' Surely the more information they had, the better? I was the only man on board not employed by the *Sudur Havid*'s owners and managers. If someone was going to describe what really happened then it should probably be me.

13:58, Tuesday, 16 June 1998

I took my seat at the table in a smart office building, on the outskirts of Stanley. The police detective in charge of the investigation, DC Jonathan Butler, had organized a meeting room as a more comfortable setting than the police station. A tape recorder and a microphone sat on the desk, much as I had expected.

I spoke at the policeman and his colleague for three hours. We started with my arrival in Cape Town on 4 April. DC Butler asked for clarification as we went along, and I tried to give as much detail as I could. They offered me a break, but now that the information was spilling out of me I did not want to stop. The tape had to be changed several times. We finished with the names of those I had seen dead.

The inquest would start the next day. I felt relieved to get the formality of the interview over, but dragging up the memories had been traumatic. I limped to the Globe Tavern, in need of a Guinness and the company of my crewmates for a distraction. I sat on a stool at the table between Brian and Mark. Hannes put some money in the jukebox, and we did our best to get drunk and forget. 'High' by The Lighthouse Family came over the sound system, it had been a surprise hit with the fishermen of the *Sudur Havid*. We sang along, and Mark burst into tears.

Friday, 19 June 1998

The Coroner's inquest took place in the Town Hall in Stanley. The spacious, formal council room gave proceedings a reassuring authority. We were asked to read out our evidence, and the Coroner asked a few questions, but there were no grand accusations or scandalous verdicts.

After three days of evidence, the formalities came to a close and we were told we were free to leave. Almost two weeks had passed since the *Sudur Havid* had sunk, and we all just wanted to see our families.

Efeinge had been admitted to hospital in Stanley, suffering chest problems from inhaling saltwater. He was recovering, but would be delayed by a few days. The rest of us were booked on the RAF flight the next day, to Brize Norton, England. We half expected a troop plane with metal benches. From there, I would go home to Aberdeen while my crewmates would transfer for another flight to Cape Town.

The *Isla Camila* appeared at anchor in the inlet just off Stanley while we were attending the inquest. Captain Sandoval had been unable to bring us directly to the Falklands, but had been forced to make the trip to pick up a new Observer. Although most of her crew weren't coming ashore, two were heading home to Chile.

On our last night in Falkland, we were out once again at the Globe Tavern. It was busy and loud, and we had been promised a party at the Town Hall disco later, above the courtroom, if our feet were up to it. I had my hand around a pint of beer. The raw patch on my ring finger was clearly visible, where I had jammed my hand so firmly behind the life-raft pillar that my skin had rubbed away on the canopy.

A Chilean man came across and started trying to talk to me. He was short and strongly built, with dark curls and a friendly smile. His face was clean-shaven, and his cheeks were rosy after his first shower ashore. He clearly had something important he wanted to say, but my Spanish was worse than his English, and I was struggling to understand. Thankfully, a woman nearby offered to step in and act as translator for us both.

Jesus Pousada, one of the *Isla Camila*'s crew, had something to ask me.

'He says, "Do you remember me?" '

'Of course, I remember you, from the *Isla Camila*.'

He looked disappointed. I must have given the wrong answer.

'Do you remember it was me who pulled you on to the boat?'

The moment was such a blur, and I was almost unconscious. I tried to explain.

'I cannot remember faces, only hands grabbing me and falling down on the deck.'

'It was me. I grabbed you with my friend and we pulled you; we stood you on your feet. And then I kissed you on your cheek and said, "Thank you, God." '

I had been thinking about how much we owed the *Isla Camila* all week. Giving evidence to the police and the Coroner's inquest had made it crystal clear just how lucky we were to be alive, and how much we owed Captain Sandoval and his crew. I fought to find the right words, through the haze of a few too many pints of beer.

'We won't forget what you did for us that night, you know?'

It was inadequate but, after a pause for translation, he nodded. If I was to make a gesture, it was now or never; I would probably never see Jesus or any of his crewmates again.

'When I have children, one day, if one is a girl, I will call her "Camila", to remind me of what you all did for us.'

EPILOGUE

16:04, Friday, 6 June 2008

I'm standing ankle-deep in cold grey seawater, on a beach just north of Aberdeen. I have an ice-cold Castle beer in each hand. The cream-and-red labels proudly declare the contents to be 'The Great South African Beer'. Dog walkers wander behind me on the golden sand. I can feel their stares. Their dogs bound down towards me, and I hope their owners don't follow. This is my private ceremony; no one joins or witnesses it, but this year will be my last. It is ten years since the sinking; time to move on.

Gazing out at the clouds on the horizon, feeling self-conscious, I speak out loud. I hope the wind will carry my words out to sea, to be heard.

'This is for you, boys. I haven't forgotten you. Another year goes by. I hope you're all resting in peace.'

Taking a swig from the bottle in my right hand, I pour a mouthful of the second beer into the water around my feet. I think that somewhere out in the ocean these drifting traces of Castle beer will eventually reach the souls of my friends and crewmates, to remind them of their homes and good times. Their real memorial, not of stone or wood but of saltwater, flows around my feet and mixes with the amber Castle.

I pause and sip from my bottle, and then pour another mouthful into the sea from the other. The cold water biting at my ankles reminds me of the deep chill I felt in the raft. I was so cold. We were so lucky.

I try to recite the names of my lost crewmates.

'Here's to you, lads: Bubbles, Boetie, Alfie, Trevor, Simon, Joaquim, Carlos, Kashingola, Grant, David, Kenny.'

The list should go on: Peinge, Melvin, Haimbodi, Kanime, Kelobi, Albert, but my memories are fading.

Finally I utter my annual incantation, my favourite words.

'There are three things I'll never forget: the laughs and the good times we had on that boat, the way everyone behaved on that day, and the *Isla Camila*, for rescuing us.'

I empty my bottle into my mouth as I pour the last of the beer in the other bottle into the sea. For the boys.

13:00, Tuesday, 28 July 2009

It's a mad sprint from our house to the maternity unit at Aberdeen Royal Infirmary. Our two-year-old son, Tate, is with our neighbour. Corinne leans heavily on my arm as we are led through to the labour ward. The delivery room is light and airy, the summer sun brightening the blinds. The midwife and her student try to put us at ease, and start to run through the paperwork, but it all happens so fast. Within twenty minutes, Corinne is giving birth. When the midwife cradles the baby in her hands, Corinne asks:

'What is it? Is it a boy or a girl?'

'It's . . . it's a girl . . . I think?' I reply, shocked and elated.

Corinne wipes the blonde hair back from her face, and smiles with joy and relief; finally, a girl. The new arrival cries.

'Does she have a name?' the midwife asks.

'She does. Camila.'

I've been waiting eleven years to say this, and to write her name: Camila. One 'l', like the boat. Eleven years to fulfil a promise.

Later I type an email to Phil Marshall, now a Fisheries Officer in Wales, to tell him of Camila's arrival:

Phil, she is a living 'Thank you' for the actions of you and your crewmates on that evening.

If it weren't for them, there would be no me, no us, no Tate, no Camila.

AFTERWORD

There were 38 of us on board the *Sudur Havid*.

In the first raft to be found, all 14 crew members survived.

In the second raft – my raft – 10 out of 17 died.

As Bjorgvin once said, 'We were seventeen. We are seven now.'

However many were in the third raft, there were no survivors, lost along with anyone else who was left in the water.

In total, 17 men never returned.

I have lost contact with almost all of the survivors. They flew back into Cape Town to be greeted by a crowd of well-wishers, friends and family, journalists' questions, newspaper and magazine articles. Some of them disappeared home, some went abroad, and others returned to sea.

When we separated at RAF Brize Norton I walked through to arrivals, and stepped back into my usual world. Corinne and I moved into a flat, and the physical work of redecorating gave me some purpose. I attended a few sessions of counselling, which helped me feel like I was addressing the event. Eventually, I took a job in a shop for a few months, just to re-establish some normality.

Within eight months, I was back at sea, proving to myself that I still enjoyed a challenge. The Spanish freezer trawler was bigger and better than the *Sudur Havid*, and the waters off Newfoundland were not as cold or as rough as the Southern Ocean. I felt fine. I could still laugh at those being seasick, still work on the wave-washed deck and still watch the spray pelting the bridge windows – all without having a panic attack.

The adrenaline rush from the accident sustained me for a year, and then the normal world came crashing back in. I was lost. I didn't have the delightful feeling that each day was a bonus. Instead, I had no idea of how to get on with the rest of my life.

In the autumn of 1999, the South African Maritime Safety Authority asked me to appear at a Court of Marine Inquiry in Cape Town. This offered me the chance to tell the story to someone who might understand, but it also gave me the opportunity to catch up with my former crewmates. The inquiry promised to be interesting: at the simple Coroner's inquest in the Falkland Islands, crew members had given conflicting stories, and those who thought that they might be apportioned some of the blame were manoeuvring awkwardly. My statement to the police in Stanley had been by far the longest and most comprehensive of anyone from our group. I wanted to find out what the South African authorities would think of it all, and wanted to help.

Who was responsible for the sinking? My opinion at the time was that the blame lay squarely with the Engineers on duty, for their lack of help with the pumps, and with the company men in South Africa, for putting us to sea in an unseaworthy vessel. Ultimately, my anger was directed at the vessel owners, for allowing such a culture to exist within the company. Curiously, I could not see the mistakes made by those in command. When the facts were examined in the cold, objective light of a courtroom, what was found did not sit easily with me at first.

The MFV *Sudurhavid* sank on the afternoon of 6 June 1998 with the loss of 17 of her crew due to the Officers on the bridge (Brian Kuttel and Gerard McDonagh) of the vessel failing to handle the vessel in a manner appropriate to the weather conditions resulting in the vessel being flooded by sea water through non watertight openings in the starboard side of the factory deck. (From the Report of the Court of Marine Inquiry)

Hard to compare as they might be, both *Titanic* and *Sudur Havid* were lost because of reckless, prideful decisions made by those in command. Captain E. J. Smith could have chosen to slow down when he heard the warnings of icebergs, in the same way that Boetie and Bubbles could have stopped fishing when the weather was so rough and sorted out the problem with the pumps. They were in charge, it was their choice, it cost them their lives and it ended and affected the lives of many others. The dead can't defend themselves, and it seems dishonourable to slight their name, particularly when they were as loved and likeable as Bubbles and Boetie. But it took a long time for me to be at ease with the idea that some of those who died were some of the most worthy of blame.

The mistakes we made

Some people say that they have 'no regrets in life'. I think this normally means that they have not recognized the harm and pain that they have caused themselves and others with their actions. I have a big bunch of regrets. I don't dwell on them, but I'd be a fool not to have recognized that certain decisions and actions have been detrimental.

There have been some people I have spoken to who have hinted that this would never have happened to them because – unlike me – they grew up with the sea, and understand it. Many of those on the *Sudur Havid* had 'grown up with the sea', and died on it. Perhaps they had spent so much time on the ocean that they had grown blasé about its risks.

I wish we had not taken on fuel in the Falklands

In the normal routine of coastal fishing, a vessel will return to port to offload her catch, and then refuel and resupply. Ten days before the accident, we had taken on fuel without removing any weight from the boat. She was heavily laden with thirty-eight men and their supplies, as well as eighty-five tonnes of fuel, eighty tonnes of fish, and many kilometres of wet rope.

Bubbles should have carried out stability calculations to determine if we were overloaded. Did she still have the 'righting moment' that would bring the boat upright after each roll? Bjorgvin, who was highly qualified and experienced, would have been able to work out the effects of taking on fuel while loaded with catch, but was not given the information or the opportunity.

In the thirty-four years since she had been built, the *Sudur Havid* had been modified from her original design – she had been added to, chopped about and changed and hatches had been cut into the factory that could not be made watertight. The water that entered through the hatches and that built up on the factory deck added the 'free-surface effect' to the ship's troubles: many tonnes of water washed from side to side with each roll, accentuating her instability and drastically altering her centre of gravity.

I wish we had stopped fishing earlier

If Bubbles and Boetie had listened to their crew and officers, when we tried to warn them, we could have stopped fishing before the problems in the factory became terminal. If they had come down to the factory they would have seen the problems. We should have attached a buoy and then cut the mainline, and retrieved it later. This would have allowed Boetie to turn the boat and shield the winch pit, which would have lessened the ingress of water, and freed other crew members to remedy the flooding. We would have lost some fish from the line, but if they had stopped fishing earlier then we might have been able to save the boat, the catch and the rest of the season.

A proper assessment of the situation may have led Bubbles and Boetie to call another vessel sooner for assistance, reducing the time for help to arrive and making success in a search more likely.

It would also have allowed them more time to prepare kit and crew for an abandon-ship.

I wish we had pushed the life-rafts around to the lee of the vessel and boarded them there

By the time I reached the life-rafts, one had already been cut loose but two were close to each other on the starboard side of the boat, pinned against the hull by the wind. This made boarding much more convenient, but if we had dragged the rafts around to the port side (and tied our painter with a releasable knot), we would have been blown away from the boat. In the few moments that we were battered against the hull and plunged underwater by the stern gantry, we were dealt a severe disadvantage that would cost the lives of over half of the men in our raft.

We don't know what happened to the occupants of the third life-raft. Were they thrown into the sea within minutes, or did they drift for hours to be rolled by a wave in the middle of the night? If the rafts had stayed together they would have been easier to find, and if they capsized we would have been in a better position to help.

The boarding of the life-rafts wasn't chaotic, and didn't degenerate into the violent squabble that some had feared, but neither was it co-ordinated. Before the accident, I had never even considered that we might one day have to abandon ship. That naivety meant that I had not even considered the best way to survive. I had no strategy.

I wish we had checked our crewmates within the raft

Bjorgvin once said, 'We were seventeen. We are seven now.'

Taking the time to check that our lifejackets were properly fitted and securely tied, while we were still on the boat (and still had dexterity), would have been minutes well spent. Many of our lifejackets had slipped or shifted; I ripped my lifejacket off as I kept getting tangled in the badly tied straps. Bodies were floating face down in our raft, and this shouldn't have happened if the lifejackets had been worn properly. If we had conducted abandon-ship drills, we would have been more familiar with their design and use.

Hypothermia takes a surprisingly long time to set in, but sudden immersion in water at $-1°C$ rendered some of our colleagues helpless in an instant, and may well have killed them outright. It is probable that many of our crewmates were killed not by hypothermia, but by drowning once they had slipped into the water. A properly fitted lifejacket would have kept their heads supported above the water and may have stopped them from drowning.

'Cold shock' is a debilitating falter in respiration and circulation, when the body reacts to the over-stimulation of cold receptors in the skin. The sudden constriction of blood vessels, and the surge of hormones released as a reaction to the stress, can cause a jump in blood pressure that can disrupt the rhythms of the heart. Such cold water can also cause a gasp for air and then a launch into hyperventilation, with all its dizziness, confusion and panic. After the shock, it doesn't take long for muscles and nerves to chill, and for a casualty to lose their co-ordination and strength.

When I was inside the raft, it was hard to think of the well-being of others once the effects of the cold and the realization of our predicament kicked in. Such introversion is also a symptom of hypothermia. But I wish we had checked that our crewmates were properly supported in the water, whether by lifejackets or by sticking their arms through the line around the edge of the life-raft. Unconscious, hypothermic casualties may have responded to rewarming on the *Isla Camila*; drowned, dead bodies would not.

I wish we had kept our boots on

Many of us shed our boots before we abandoned ship, fearing that any hooks lodged into their soles might damage the rafts, and that our ability to swim could be affected. I am not convinced that we had many hooks embedded in our boots. I am, however, certain that if we had kept them on, they would have provided a much better seal for preventing water from circulating in and out of our trousers, and would have therefore preserved vital body heat.

I forced myself out of the water, straddling the rope, but most of my colleagues were submerged in water up to their chests. Although they may have felt warmer by avoiding any wind and evaporative cooling, the water would have been stripping the warmth from their bodies much faster than the air.

Since the accident, the only physical repercussion of the sinking that I experience is a lack of control of the circulation in my feet. The short time in freezing water was enough to damage the tissue and blood vessels, which is known as 'immersion foot', or if acquired on land 'trench foot'. For Morné, the symptoms included his legs swelling to twice their normal size and the skin tearing from his feet. Bjorgvin suffered full frostbite, with tissue that died and wounds that took months to heal.

The shedding of our boots was symptomatic of our inadequate survival knowledge, strategy and preparation. Those of us in the factory did not have long to prepare, between leaving the attempts to save the boat and boarding the rafts, but I still had time to find my deck-suit. Many of us could have donned more clothes, more layers and more protection. Survival experts recommend dressing in extra layers before abandoning ship, and then wearing a properly fastened lifejacket.

I wish we had been better equipped, and used the equipment available properly

One raft did not inflate, while my own raft was damaged and malfunctioning. The design made the doors hard to close against the weather. Vital kit – bailers, sea anchor, light – was missing or had been lost during our battering. No one seemed familiar with the deployment or operation of the rafts, including the supposedly experienced officers.

I am eternally grateful for my deck-suit. Without it, I am

convinced that I would have died. My chances would have been even better had I been wearing a full immersion suit. Properly sealed, it would have protected me from the cold-water shock of the first few minutes and would have kept me warmer for longer. What chance did Simon have? Used to the heat of the galley, he abandoned ship barefoot in a T-shirt.

I wish we had been able to recover all of the bodies from our raft, and slowly rewarm them

By the time I was pulled from the raft, I was barely able to look after myself, and was in no state to assist in the recovery of the casualties, unconscious or dead. The same goes for all my raft-mates.

No one could have expected the crew of the *Isla Camila* to have risked their lives even further by descending into the raft, particularly in the conditions that day and without any proper equipment. But I wish that, somehow, we had been able to recover all ten of our colleagues, instead of four, on to the *Isla Camila*. Maybe Bubbles or one of the other silent casualties was just unconscious? There was the chance that one of them might have responded to slow and proper rewarming, and regained consciousness.

In addition to the heart attack that he may have suffered as we abandoned the boat, Bubbles might have been a victim of one aspect of rescue collapse. Once rescue seems possible, and hope replaces fear, the body can stop releasing the stress hormones that protect the heart during hypothermia – and the casualty suffers heart failure. If this was the case, even rewarming wouldn't have helped him.

Most of all I wish we had not gone fishing

The few weeks we spent fishing were unforgettable, and I feel lucky to have met the men of the *Sudur Havid*. Ultimately, however, I wish that we had stayed at home and had not gone fishing. It wasn't worth it. With our poor preparation and decisions, we were lucky that anyone survived at all.

REPORT OF THE COURT OF MARINE INQUIRY: THE SINKING OF THE MFV *SUDURHAVID*

[This is an extract from the report of the Court of Marine Inquiry, ordered by the Minister of Transport in South Africa, and released on 6 December 1999. There are some discrepancies between these findings and my and other eyewitness accounts.]

The court is required:

QUESTION 1:

To ascertain what the facts and circumstances were surrounding the sinking of the MFV *Sudurhavid* on or about 6 June 1998.

ANSWER:

The *Sudurhavid* sank at approximately 16:00 local time (18:00 GMT) on the 6th of June 1998 in the Southern Atlantic off the South Georgia Islands at a position approximately 53° 45′ South, 45° 13′ West while performing long line fishing for Patagonian Toothfish in adverse weather conditions and deteriorating, with wind at Force 7 and increasing, and the wave height at six metres or more. Due to the fact that the vessel was low in the water and had openings in the starboard side plating, that could not be made watertight, the vessel became more vulnerable to flooding. The vessel rolled in high seas causing water to build up on the factory deck, the wash of this water caused fish offal to enter the dills and being drawn into the pumps causing the pumps to be unable to cope with the ingress of water. The reserve pumps could not be utilized timeously. The water on the factory deck eventually caused the vessel to an angle of loll to starboard causing the sea to have free access into the hull. The vessel eventually lay on her starboard side and subsequently filled the lower decks, causing her to sink as a direct result of ingress of water into the hull.

QUESTION 2:

To ascertain what the cause or causes were of the sinking of the MFV *Sudurhavid* on or about 6 June 1998.

ANSWER:

The following matters caused or contributed to the sinking of the *Sudurhavid* on 6 June 1998:

1. The excessive quantities of sea water entering the vessel in heavy weather whilst the boat was longlining. More specifically the vessel had an increased draft on this day and was therefore more vulnerable to seawater ingress especially in the heavy sea conditions. The long-line fishing gear acted to hold the vessel's starboard side to the weather. The side had openings penetrating the hull above the factory deck.

2. The modifications to the starboard side of the vessel were not watertight. This fact invalidated the existing stability booklet.

3. The owners did not professionally check that the modifications were watertight but relied on the statutory SAMSA [South African Maritime Safety Authority] surveys.

4. The vessel was allowed to sail without the stability information being checked and updated.

5. In worsening weather the inflow of sea water through the fish chute increased.

6. Until this stage the pumps were coping with the water. The size of the pumps was not particularly significant.

7. The additional water coming through the openings in the starboard side washed the offal out of the bins which blocked the pumps and dill gratings.

8. The pumps were difficult to clean and the water level built up on the factory deck. This would have been so

whatever make of pumps or method of installation was used.

9. The electrical auxiliary pump was unserviceable due to the fact that it could not be quickly connected to a power socket.

10. The emergency diesel pump, which had not been tested and started regularly, could not be started in the cold conditions prevailing.

11. The third new electric pump was not ready for use.

12. The officers conning the vessel on the afternoon of 6 June 1998 failed to take timeous action to cut the long-line or to bring the vessel's head up into the weather. This caused the vessel to roll into the high seas and to scoop water into the factory deck through non-watertight openings on the starboard side. Due to the increased inflow of water on the factory deck the vessel took an angle of loll, to starboard, which exacerbated the inflow from seaward which eventually found its way to the lower levels in the vessel, causing the *Sudurhavid* to sink.

QUESTION 3:

To ascertain whether any person or persons, whether natural or juristic, and whether directly or indirectly, and whether by any act or omission, was or were at fault in any way for this aforementioned sinking.

ANSWER:

We find that the officers Gerard John McDonagh and Brian Christopher Kuttel, on the bridge of the *Sudurhavid* during the afternoon of 6 June 1998 were at fault in that they failed to handle the vessel in a manner appropriate to the prevailing weather conditions resulting in the vessel sinking.

Although this was the direct cause we find that the following matters contributed to the tragic event. With regard to:

1. City Fishing [vessel owners]:

   (a) The employment of Captain Armannsson for the sole purpose of meeting statutory certification requirements.

   (b) Allowing the *Sudurhavid* to proceed on this voyage with unsatisfactory watertight integrity which compromised her seaworthiness in conditions that she could be expected to encounter during the voyage.

2. Aluship [vessel managers]:

   (a) We are concerned about the casual attitude of Aluship in managing the vessel.

   (b) Our concern is borne out by the manner in which Captain Armannsson, Kuttel and McDonagh were contracted; the application for the correct exemptions to SAMSA; the use of shoreside personnel without adequate marine expertise; allowing modifications to the vessel without taking cognisance of the watertightness of the vessel and the lack of application of standing orders and drills.

3. SAMSA: [South African Maritime Safety Authority]

   (a) We find that SAMSA was in error in allowing the vessel to sail without approved documentation, eg. Failing to record the change of master; no approved stability booklet on board at the time of sailing as well as the lack of a tonnage certificate.

   (b) We are concerned that a Local General Safety Certificate was issued whilst the above was not done.

4. Mr Alan Newman:

   (a) The actions of Newman, being the manager of the vessel, specifically regarding the employment of Armannsson, as master, were improperly done.

(b) Being the manager of the vessel, Newman himself did not take appropriate steps in respect to the replacement of the pumps.

5. Armannsson:

(a) We find that Capt Armannsson should have clarified his position on board of the vessel with the owners and, if in fact appointed master, should have exerted his authority throughout the voyage.

6. Kuttel and McDonagh:

(a) They ignored the specific instructions of the owners with regard to the position of Captain Armannsson and effectively held command and control of the vessel.

7. Engineers:

(a) We find that the Chief Engineer lacked diligence in that he failed to ensure that the diesel emergency pump was run on a regular basis during the voyage in order to ensure that it will be ready for use in the case of an emergency.

QUESTION 4:

To ascertain what the facts and circumstances were surrounding the loss of 17 crew members following upon or during the sinking of the MFV *Sudurhavid* on or about 6 June 1998.

ANSWER:

When it became clear that the vessel was going to sink, the crew decided to abandon their ship. Lifejackets which were stored in a locker were handed out. No immersion suits were available for the crew. The observer and Armannsson however did have their own. Four life-rafts were launched. One became damaged and did not inflate. All members of the crew got into the remaining three life-rafts. A life-raft with seven crew members was swept away and later found empty. The seven crew members that were in it were never found and must be assumed dead. A life-raft with ten crew members as retrieved about four and a half hours later by the *Isla Camila* and all the crew in it were rescued. A liferaft with 17 crew on board was hit by the aft gantry of the *Sudurhavid* which damaged the raft causing it to be flooded but it remained afloat. Ten of the crew who boarded it were rescued by the *Isla Camila*. The other seven crew members who boarded it were either dead or missing when the raft was retrieved.

QUESTION 5:

To ascertain what the cause or causes were of the loss of life of 17 crew members following upon the or during the sinking of the MFV *Sudurhavid* on or about 6 June 1998.

ANSWER:

After abandoning the *Sudurhavid* all of the crew members embarked into three life-rafts. Due to the cold wind and sea conditions exposure was a major factor with reference to survival. One of the life-rafts with seven persons aboard was swept away and was later found empty. The bodies were never recovered. Due to the conditions prevailing it must be presumed that all of the occupants died. One of the life-rafts, with 17 people in it, was struck by the *Sudurhavid*'s aft gantry which caused the raft to flood. The entrapped cold sea water in the liferaft would have caused accelerated hypothermia of its occupants. As no post mortem evidence was available to the court in respect of any of the deceased one may only speculate that the cause of death of the deceased was most probably hypothermia.

QUESTION 6:

To ascertain whether any person or persons, whether natural or juristic, directly or indirectly, and whether by any act or omission, was or were at fault for the loss of life of 17 crew members following upon or during the aforementioned sinking.

ANSWER:

As determined in question 3 we find that the officers on the bridge of the vessel (Gerard John McDonagh and Brian Christopher Kuttel) failed to handle the vessel appropriate to the prevailing conditions, which ultimately led to the sinking of the vessel with consequent loss of life.

QUESTION 7 – Considered a matter of a point of law

Report of a Court of Marine Inquiry:

The court having carefully inquired into the circumstances attending the matter to be investigated, finds for the reasons stated in our oral judgement, that the MFV *Sudurhavid* sank on the afternoon of 6 June 1998 with the loss of 17 of her crew due to the officers on the bridge of the vessel failing to handle her in a manner appropriate to the prevailing weather conditions resulting in the vessel being flooded through non watertight openings in the starboard side of the factory deck.

SELECT BIBLIOGRAPHY

Carr, Tim and Pauline. *Antarctic Oasis*. W. W. Norton and Company, 1998

Golden, Frank, and Michael Tipton. *Essentials of Sea Survival*. Human Kinetics, 2002

Howorth, Frances, and Michael Howorth. *The Sea Survival Manual*. Adlard Coles Nautical, 2005

Shirihai, Hadoram. *A Complete Guide to Antarctic Wildlife*. A&C Black, 2007